A+ PROJECTS & DIORAMAS
The Student's Handbook

A division of Woodland Scenics®

Woodland Scenics
PO Box 98
Linn Creek, MO 65052
woodlandscenics.com

Printed and bound in the U.S.A.

Copyright ©2010 O CO

ISBN-13: 978-1-887436-15-1
ISBN-10: 1-887436-15-4

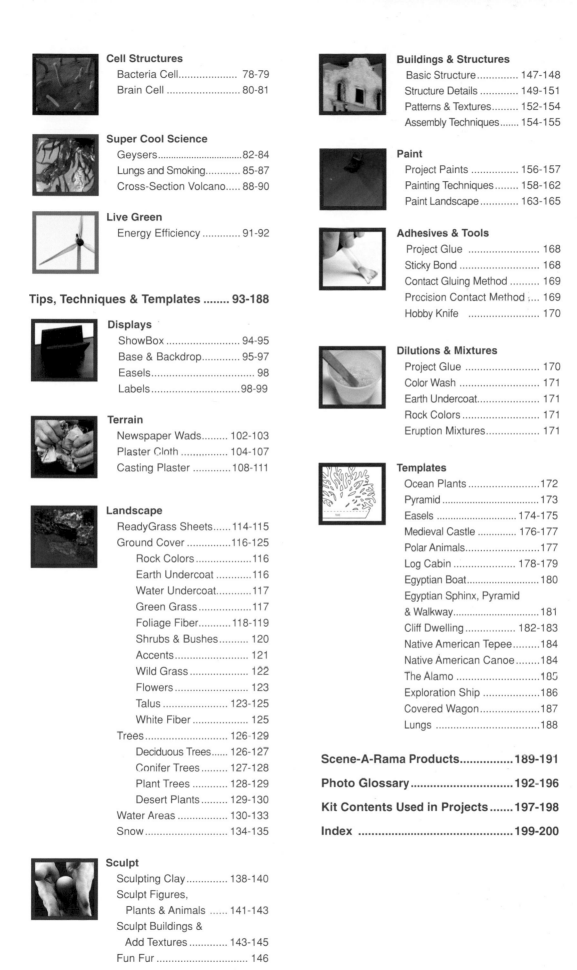

Welcome to Scene-A-Rama!

When homework is fun, you learn more, understand better and remember longer. Scene-A-Rama makes it easy to have fun, get creative and let your imagination run wild! Design and create one-of-a-kind school projects, dioramas and displays or just have fun with arts and crafts at home. Making projects is simple with the easy-to-use materials that work together to create virtually anything you want.

The Students Handbook to A⁺ Projects and Dioramas is a Complete Resource!

In the first section, you will find colorful step-by-step, illustrated instructions to make 34 different projects for science, social studies, history and other subjects. The projects in this handbook represent commonly studied school subjects. You can complete a project exactly as presented or easily change it to fit your assignment and your imagination!

The Tips, Techniques & Templates section shows you more than 250 ways to use Scene-A-Rama materials. Learning these simple techniques is key to using the materials. Once you know the techniques, you can apply them to other projects or make changes to one of the illustrated examples in order to fit your needs. Find more project ideas along with instructional videos at scenearama.com.

Getting Started

Once you know your topic, have done your research and decided what project you want to make, the rest is easy:

- Read through the step-by-step instructions before you begin a project. This will give you an understanding of the project and its requirements.

- Collect all needed materials.

- Prepare a clean, flat work surface. Cover your project area with newspapers or appropriate table coverings.

- If you will use materials that may stain, wear old clothing or a project smock.

- Many projects and modeling techniques suggest the use of a hobby knife. Use with caution.

- When cutting is required, use a safe, stable cutting surface.

- Get creative and have fun!

- Once your project is complete, gather all left over materials and store for your next project.

Step-by-Step Project Information

Below is an example of a project! Each project contains a lot of information, including what items we used to make the diorama and the important techniques used to complete specific steps. You will also find some fun, educational facts about the subject. Before you read further, please review this example to become familiar with the handbook's layout.

Scene-A-Rama Items
The Scene-A-Rama items used to make the dioramas are listed at the beginning of each project. Throughout the instructions, these items are capitalized and italicized for easy identification. The size of Project Base & Backdrop is also listed. Feel free to substitute the large or small size depending on your preference, but modify project materials accordingly.

Project Category
The projects are classified into 14 popular subjects. The subject groups are color coded for easy identification.

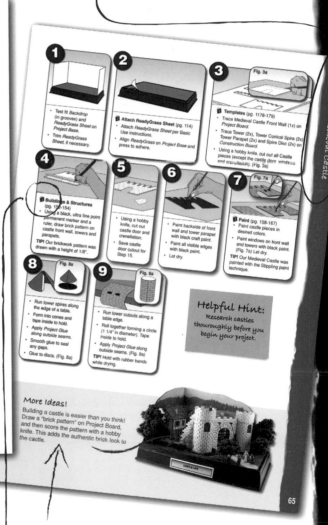

Household Items
Household items are easy-to-find materials we used to complete each project. Feel free to use additional or different items depending on your project requirements. There is more than one way to build any diorama.

ℹ️ Tips, Techniques & Templates Icon
This icon directs you to the technique you will use to complete the step. Turn to the page number(s) listed next to the technique name.

More Ideas
Following some step-by-step projects, you will find more project ideas! These ideas are for enhancing a diorama or building an entirely different project using the same Scene-A-Rama materials and techniques.

You will find product ◇Cautions and ♥Modeling and Care Information in the Photo Glossary on pages 192-196.

Tips, Techniques & Templates Information

Below are examples from the Tips, Techniques & Templates section. This section teaches you the basic modeling techniques you will use to build your project with Scene-A-Rama and household items. It also provides a variety of additional modeling techniques and tips to spark your imagination and inspire your creativity.

Main Sections
Tips, Techniques & Templates is divided into nine sections. Each section represents a different stage in the modeling process. Sections range from adhesives and tools to landscape and templates.

Subsections
Each main section is divided into subsections. Subsections include step-by-step instructions for specific modeling techniques using household and Scene-A-Rama items.

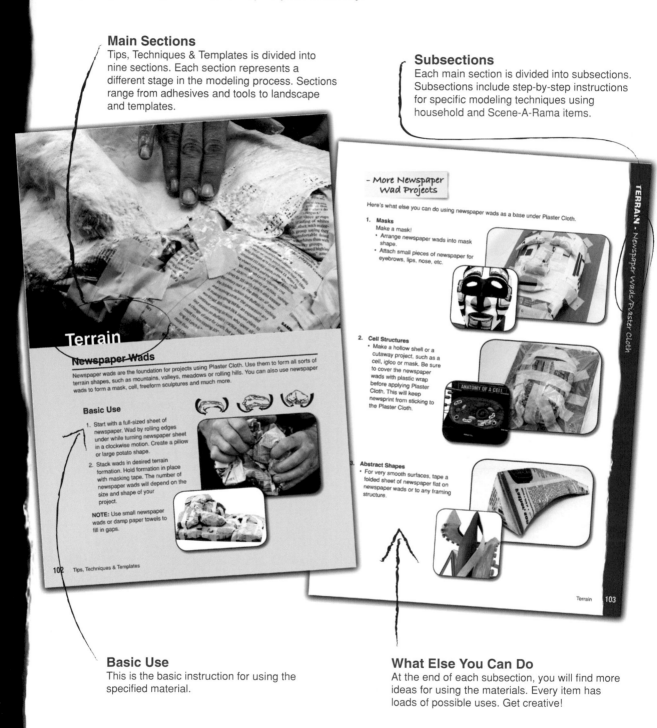

TERRAIN · Newspaper Wads/Plaster Cloth

Terrain

Newspaper Wads

Newspaper wads are the foundation for projects using Plaster Cloth. Use them to form all sorts of terrain shapes, such as mountains, valleys, meadows or rolling hills. You can also use newspaper wads to form a mask, cell, freeform sculptures and much more.

Basic Use

1. Start with a full-sized sheet of newspaper. Wad by rolling edges under while turning newspaper sheet in a clockwise motion. Create a pillow or large potato shape.
2. Stack wads in desired terrain formation. Hold formation in place with masking tape. The number of newspaper wads will depend on the size and shape of your project.

NOTE: Use small newspaper wads or damp paper towels to fill in gaps.

102   Tips, Techniques & Templates

- More Newspaper Wad Projects

Here's what else you can do using newspaper wads as a base under Plaster Cloth.

1. **Masks**
   Make a mask!
   - Arrange newspaper wads into mask shape.
   - Attach small pieces of newspaper for eyebrows, lips, nose, etc.

2. **Cell Structures**
   - Make a hollow shell or a cutaway project, such as a cell, igloo or mask. Be sure to cover the newspaper wads with plastic wrap before applying Plaster Cloth. This will keep newsprint from sticking to the Plaster Cloth.

3. **Abstract Shapes**
   - For very smooth surfaces, tape a folded sheet of newspaper flat on newspaper wads or to any framing structure.

Terrain   103

Basic Use
This is the basic instruction for using the specified material.

What Else You Can Do
At the end of each subsection, you will find more ideas for using the materials. Every item has loads of possible uses. Get creative!

You will find product ◇Cautions and ♥Modeling and Care Information in the Photo Glossary on pages 192-196.

Step-by-Step
PROJECTS &
DIORAMAS

AQUARIUM

Here's what we used...

SCENE A RAMA® Items

- **Sculpting Kit**
- **Scene Setters: Marine Life**
- **Desert Sand ReadyGrass Sheet**
- **ShowBox**

Household Items

- Disposable Cup
- Foam Brush (1")
- Newspaper
- Pencil
- Rubber Bands
- Ruler
- Scissors
- White Paper (2)

Did you know?

An aquarium is a tank with at least one glass side for keeping and exhibiting aquatic plants and animals. Aquariums come in all shapes and sizes. There are small ones, like ones found in homes, to very large ones housing dolphins and whales at marine mammal parks.

Fun Fact!
Sperm Whales can hold their breath up to 40 minutes!

AQUARIUM

1

ℹ ShowBox (pg. 94) and **Paint** (pg. 156-165)
- Assemble *ShowBox*.
- Paint an underwater scene inside your *ShowBox*.
- Paint the outside if desired.
- Let dry.

2

ℹ ReadyGrass Sheets (pg. 114)
- Measure and cut *ReadyGrass Sheet* to fit bottom of *ShowBox*.
- Glue in place using *Project Glue*.

NOTE: Save remaining *ReadyGrass* for Step 4.

3

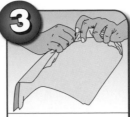

ℹ Newspaper Wads (pg. 102)
- Wad small sections of newspaper to make sea rocks.
- You choose the size, shape and number of rocks.

4

Fig. 4a

- Cut sections of *ReadyGrass* to fit around newspaper wads.
- Use *Project Glue* to glue in place. Use rubber bands to hold shape while drying. (Fig. 4a)

TIP! When making rocks, some *Desert Sand* may fall off. Glue it on the sea floor to add realistic textures.

5

Fig. 5a

ℹ Ocean Plants Template (pg. 172)
- Use templates to draw sea plants on white paper in a variety of heights and widths or use included templates.
- Paint as desired. (Fig. 5a)
- Set aside to dry. Then, cut out.

TIP! Curl sea plants using a pencil. This will give them a realistic shape.

6

ℹ Sculpt Figures, Plants & Animals (pg. 138-142)
- Sculpt sea life (coral, sea vegetation, animals, etc.).
- Paint as desired.
- Set aside to dry

TIP! Scenearama.com has How-to Videos.

7

Fig. 7a

- Design your aquarium. Decide where to put marine animals, vegetation and rocks.
- Glue vegetation, loose *Desert Sand* and rocks in place. (Fig. 7a)

8

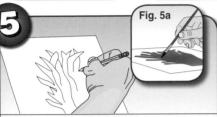

- Use *Project Glue* to install *Scene Setters*.
- For swimming animals, cut *Project Wire* to desired length and attach to *Scene Setters*. Glue opposite end to desired location.

TIP! Have a grown-up help you with this step.

9

ℹ Labels (pg. 98-99)
- Label and add signage to your project.

Helpful Hint
Small seashells or other items from nature add authentic details.

More Ideas!

Are you feeling creative? Try sculpting marine life figures! It's easy with Sculpting Clay and Project Paints from the Scene-A-Rama Sculpting Kit.

COASTAL TIDE POOL

Here's what we used...

SCENE A RAMA® Items

- **Water Diorama Kit**
- **Sculpting Kit**
- **Small Project Base & Backdrop**

Household Items

- Cutting Surface
- Disposable Cups
- Hobby Knife
- Masking Tape
- Newspaper
- Pan for Water
- Scissors
- Small Seashells

Did you know?

Tide pools are rocky areas next to the ocean that fill up with seawater during high tide. During low tide, many unique and beautiful animals are visible. You could find sea stars, sea anemones, mussels, urchins, crabs and kelp, just to name a few.

COASTAL TIDE POOL

1

- Make a cardboard pad. Measure and cut a piece of cardboard *Side Panel* 10 3/8" x 7 1/8". You will build your diorama on this pad.

2

- Test fit *Backdrop* (in grooves) and cardboard pad on *Project Base*.
- Set aside *Project Base & Backdrop*.

3
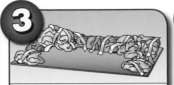
Newspaper Wads (pg. 102)
- Arrange newspaper wads on cardboard pad into desired tide pool shape.
- Tape newspaper wads in place.

NOTE: Newspaper wads must NOT protrude over sides of cardboard pad.

4

- Using newspaper wads, create additional rocks for middle of tide pool.
- Tape to hold.

TIP! See our diorama for ideas.

5 Fig. 5a

Plaster Cloth (pg. 104-105)
- Cover diorama with wet *Plaster Cloth* (3" strips), bumpy side up.
- Add 2 layers of *Plaster Cloth*.
- Overlap edges by 1/2". (Fig. 5a)

NOTE: Holes in *Plaster Cloth* will let *Realistic Water* leak through to cardboard pad (Step 13).

6

- While *Plaster Cloth* is damp, test fit on *Project Base* with *Backdrop* in grooves.
- If it interferes with the *Backdrop*, make adjustments.
- Remove from *Project Base* and let dry.

7

Earth Undercoat (pg. 171)
- Brush diluted *Earth Undercoat* over entire *Plaster Cloth* terrain.
- Let dry.

8 Fig. 8a

Project Glue in Spray Bottle (pg. 170)
- Spray diluted *Project Glue* on "algae" areas.
- Sprinkle *Green Grass* over glue until satisfied with "greenish" look. (Fig. 8a)
- Spray again to seal.

9

Ground Cover (pg. 116-121)
- Sprinkle additional colors of *Accents* as desired. Spray with diluted *Project Glue*.
- Add additional landscape materials (*Foliage Fiber* and *Shrubs*), if desired.

10

Talus (pg. 123-125)
- Spray diluted *Project Glue* on desired "rock debris" areas.
- Sprinkle *Talus* over glue.
- Spray additional diluted *Project Glue* on top of *Talus*.

TIP! Crush *Talus* into a sand.

11
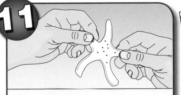
Sculpt (pg. 141-142)
- Using *Sculpting Clay*, sculpt sea creatures and plant life.
- Paint in desired colors with *Project Paints*.
- Let dry.

TIP! Go to scenearama.com and visit How-to Videos for sculpting ideas

12

- Use *Project Glue* to attach sea creatures and plants in desired locations.
- Let dry overnight.

TIP! Attach sea-shells.

13

Realistic Water (pg. 130-132)
- Pour *Realistic Water* slowly into bottom of tide pool water area.
- Let dry until clear (approx. 24 hours).

14

Project Base & Backdrop (pg. 95-97)
- Design a backdrop that fits your diorama.

15

Labels (pg. 98-99)
- Attach *Backdrop* and tide pool to *Project Base* using *Project Glue*.
- Make sure the label area faces forward.
- Label your project and add signage.

Fun Fact!
Marine scientists are giving the starfish a new name: Sea Star. Why? The Sea Star is not a fish. It is an echinoderm, closely related to sea urchins.

GLACIERS & ICEBERGS

Here's what we used...

SCENE A RAMA® Items

- **Winter Effects**
- **Ripplin' Water Kit**
- **Plaster Cloth**
- **Small Project Base & Backdrop**

Household Items

- Corrugated Cardboard, 11" x 15"
- Craft Paints and Brushes
- Cutting Surface
- Disposable Cup
- Hobby Knife
- Masking Tape
- Newspaper
- Pan for Water
- Pencil
- Ruler
- Scissors

Did you know?

Glaciers form when more snow falls in the winter than melts in the summer. The weight of new snow falling on top of old snow causes it to compact into dense snow, which slowly turns into thick, white glacier ice. Glaciers are found in high mountains and near the North and South Poles.

Icebergs are large floating chunks of fresh-water ice that break off or calve (KAHV) from land-based glaciers and free-float in the open ocean.

Fun Fact!

The largest recorded iceberg is labeled B-15. It had an area approximately 11,000 km². That's larger than the island of Jamaica!

Did You Know...
Caribou /Reindeer are almost constantly on the move. They migrate more than 3,000 miles per year
Did You Know...
The Emperor Penguin is the largest of all penguins, standing approx. 4 ft. and they are the only penguins that breed in the winter.
Did You Know...
The Sea Lion is the most trained "seal", used by zoos and aquariums. They are also the largest of the eared seals
Did You Know...
Polar Bears spend many months of the year at sea. They have hollow hair and black skin to help keep them warm, and they never drink water.
Did You Know...
The Walrus is the largest of the pinnipeds (meaning web-footed),they can run on all fours as fast as a man. The males tusk can reach 4 ft. in length.

GLACIERS & ICEBERGS

1

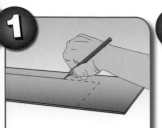

- Make a cardboard pad. Measure and cut a piece of cardboard 10-3/8" x 7-1/8". You will build your diorama on this pad.

2

- Test fit *Backdrop* (in grooves) and cardboard pad on *Project Base*.
- Set aside.

3

Fig. 3a

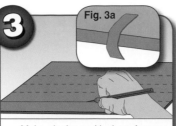

- Make glacier and iceberg forms.
- Using a pencil and ruler, draw 1/2" wide strips on a separate piece of cardboard.
- Cut out with a hobby knife.
- Run strips along the edge of a table so they are easy to shape. (Fig. 3a)

4

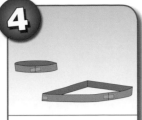

- Cut strips to desired lengths.
- Form strips into preferred glacier and iceberg shapes and tape to hold.

5

Fig. 5a

ℹ Newspaper Wads (pg. 102)

- Tape forms in desired locations on cardboard.
- Fill forms with newspaper wads and tape to hold shape.
- For flat topped glaciers and icebergs: place masking tape strips across top of forms. (Fig. 5a)

6

Fig. 6a

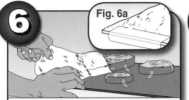

ℹ Plaster Cloth (pg. 104-105)

- Cover with wet *Plaster Cloth* (3" strips), bumpy side up.
- Add two layers of *Plaster Cloth*.
- Overlap edges by 1/2". (Fig. 6a)

NOTE: Holes in *Plaster Cloth* will let *Realistic Water* leak through to cardboard pad (Step 11).

7

Lip

- Using thin, wet *Plaster Cloth* strips, build a small lip around the outer edge of cardboard.
- Pinch to shape.

8

- While *Plaster Cloth* is damp, test fit on *Project Base* with *Backdrop* in grooves.
- Make adjustments, if needed.
- Remove from *Base*.
- Weigh down while drying to keep flat.

9

Fig 9a

ℹ Snow (pg. 134-135)

- Mix *Snow Base* and *Snowflakes* in disposable cup.
- Dab snow mixture on glacier and icebergs.
- Sprinkle additional *Snowflakes* while wet. (Fig. 9a)
- Let dry.

10

- Paint water area with *Water Undercoat*.
- Let dry.

TIP! The darker the paint color, the deeper the water will appear.

11

ℹ Realistic Water (pg. 130)

- Pour *Realistic Water* slowly on water area.
- Pull out to edges with a paintbrush or *Stir Stick*.
- Let dry until clear (approx. 24 hours).

12

ℹ Water Effects (pg. 132)

- Use *Water Effects* to add "waves" on top of dried *Realistic Water*.
- Dab on using the *Stir Stick*.
- Let dry until clear.

13

ℹ Backdrop (pg. 95-97)

- Design a *Backdrop* that best fits your diorama.
- Cut out with a hobby knife.

TIP! See our diorama for ideas.

14

ℹ Paint (pg. 156-165)

- Use craft paints (or markers) to color your *Backdrop*.

15

ℹ Polar Animals (pg. 177)

- Add animals from Template section.
- Color animals to add interest and realism.
- Attach with *Project Glue*.

16

ℹ Labels (pg. 98-99)

- Attach *Backdrop* and diorama to *Project Base* using *Project Glue*.
- Make sure the label area faces forward.
- Label and add signage to your project.

ICEBERGS

Here's what we used...

SCENE A RAMA Items

- **Winter Effects**
- **Ripplin' Water Kit**
- **Plaster Cloth**
- **Project Glue**
- **Small Project Base & Backdrop**

Household Items

- Corrugated Cardboard, 10" x 12"
- Craft Paints & Brushes
- Craft Wire
- Cutting Surface
- Disposable Cups
- Hobby Knife
- Masking Tape
- Miniature Whale
- Newspaper
- Pan for Water
- Pencil
- Scissors

Did you know?

Icebergs are large floating chunks of fresh-water ice that break off from land-based glaciers and float out to sea. Some icebergs are over one hundred feet high. They are able to float because the density of the ice at their core is lighter than the ocean water that surrounds them.

Fun Fact!

You may be surprised to learn that approximately one-eighth of an iceberg is above the waterline. Most of its mass sits in the seawater.

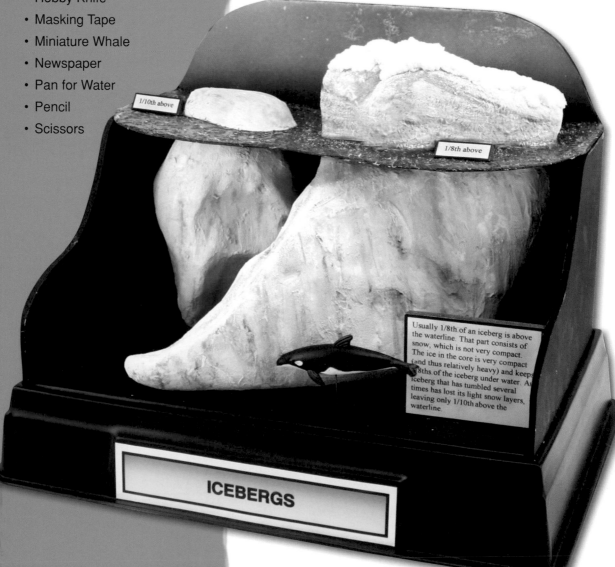

1/10th above

1/8th above

Usually 1/8th of an iceberg is above the waterline. That part consists of snow, which is not very compact. The ice in the core is very compact (and thus relatively heavy) and keeps 7/8ths of the iceberg under water. An iceberg that has tumbled several times has lost its light snow layers, leaving only 1/10th above the waterline.

ICEBERGS

1
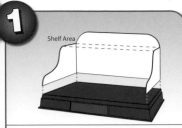

- Design a *Backdrop* using *Backdrop* material.
- Include a level shelf area for waterline.
- Cut out using a hobby knife.
- Test fit *Backdrop* in grooves on *Project Base*.

2
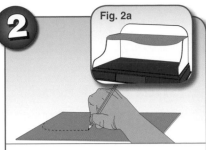

Fig. 2a

- Draw waterline pattern on cardboard.
- Cut out using a hobby knife.
- Test fit on *Backdrop*. (Fig. 2a)

3
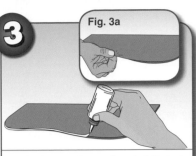

Fig. 3a

- Apply a continuous bead of *Project Glue* along front edge of waterline.
- Smooth glue into edge and pinch to create a smooth, flat surface. (Fig. 3a)

4

ℹ️ **Paint** (pg. 158-167)
- Paint waterline with *Water Undercoat*.
- Paint *Backdrop* as desired.

TIP! For an illusion of depth, paint the *Backdrop* black below the waterline.

5

Fig. 5a

ℹ️ **Newspaper Wads** (pg. 102)
- Arrange newspaper wads into 2-part iceberg shapes (Part 1: above waterline, Part 2: below waterline).
- Use masking tape to hold shape.
- Form a flat area for attaching to waterline.

NOTE: Test fit Icebergs between waterline and *Project Base*. (Fig. 5a)

6

Fig. 6a

ℹ️ **Plaster Cloth** (pg. 104-105)
- Cover newspaper wads with wet *Plaster Cloth* (3" strips), bumpy side up.
- Add 2 layers of *Plaster Cloth*.
- Pinch wet *Plaster Cloth* to create texture on iceberg surface. (Fig. 6a)
- Let dry.

7

ℹ️ **Snow Mixture** (pg. 134)
- Paint icebergs with craft paints.
- Mix *Snow Base* and *Snowflakes* in a disposable cup.
- Dab snow mixture on top of icebergs.
- Using *Plastic Cup and Sifter Lid*, sprinkle additional *Snowflakes* while wet. Let dry.

8
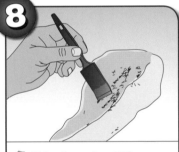

ℹ️ **Shiny Areas** (pg. 132)
- Brush *Realistic Water* over the iceberg sections that set below the waterline.

9
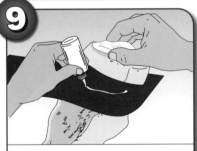

ℹ️ **Contact Gluing Method** (pg. 169)
- Use *Project Glue* to attach iceberg sections to waterline.
- Let dry.

10

- Use *Project Glue* to attach *Backdrop* to *Project Base* (label area facing forward).
- Glue waterline with icebergs to *Backdrop*.
- Let dry.

11

ℹ️ **Water Effects** (pg. 132)
- Dab *Water Effects* on top of dried *Realistic Water* using the *Stir Stick*. Let dry until clear (approx. 24 hours).

12

- Add a whale to define the scale of the icebergs.
- Display whale on a piece of craft wire or glue to *Project Base*.

13

ℹ️ **Labels** (pg. 98-99)
- Label and add signage to your project.

IGLOO LIFE

Here's what we used...

SCENE·A·RAMA® Items

- **Winter Effects**
- **Plaster Cloth**
- **Small Project Base & Backdrop**

Household Items

- Modeling Clay
- Balloon, 7"
- Bowl
- Corrugated Cardboard, 8" x 11"
- Cardstock, 8" x 10"
- Craft Paints & Brushes
- Disposable Cups
- Cutting Surface
- Foil
- Hobby Knife
- Masking Tape
- Pan for Water
- Pencil
- Scissors
- Silver Pencil

Did you know?

Do you think igloos are cool? Actually, they are very warm, considering their surroundings. The outside temperature during a harsh arctic winter can fall to -49°F. However, body heat alone can raise the temperature inside an igloo to 61°F. Because they are one of the best shelters against arctic conditions, igloos are used by indigenous hunters of Canada's Central Arctic and Greenland's Thule regions.

Fun Fact!

The blocks of packed snow or ice used to build an igloo average 24" long x 20" wide x 4" thick.

The Igloo

A recognizable form, the most unique structure to be designed by indigenous architects has to be the igloo. Constructed of packed ice and snow, this domed structure has remained unchanged for thousands of years. Although it has been misrepresented as a permanent facet of the artic communities, the igloo is actually a temporary house built when away from home, on hunting or fishing trips.

IGLOO LIFE

1

- Make a cardboard pad. Measure and cut a piece of cardboard 10-3/8" x 7-1/8". You will build your diorama on this pad.

2 Fig. 2a

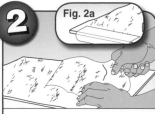

- ℹ️ **Plaster Cloth** (pg. 104-105)
- Cover cardboard pad with wet *Plaster Cloth* (3" strips), bumpy side up.
- Smooth out plaster with wet fingers to fill holes in *Cloth*.
- Overlap edges of cardboard by 1/2". (Fig. 2a)

3

- While *Plaster Cloth* is damp, test fit on *Project Base*.
- If it interferes with *Backdrop*, make adjustments.
- Remove from *Base*.
- Weigh down at corners while drying.

4

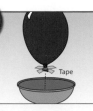
Tape

- Blow up a balloon nearly full and tie a knot. (Have an adult help you with this step.) Test fit size on *Base*.
- Tape balloon to the bottom of a shallow bowl.
- This will keep the balloon in place while applying *Plaster Cloth*.

5

- Arrange foil around the balloon to secure in place.
- Place masking tape level around the middle of the balloon.
- This will keep the igloo even along the bottom.

6

- ℹ️ **Plaster Cloth** (pg. 104-105)
- Fold a strip of *Plaster Cloth* in half, lengthwise (bumpy side out), then dip in water.
- Place on balloon using masking tape as a guide to keep igloo level along bottom.
- Lay a wet Strip of *Plaster Cloth* across the top to create an opening for cutaway view.

7

- Fill in igloo shape with strips of wet *Plaster Cloth*.
- Add 2 layers of *Plaster Cloth*.
- Let dry for approximately 15 minutes.
- Remove igloo from balloon carefully.
- Dispose of balloon immediately.

8

- When slightly damp, use a hobby knife to cut an opening for cutaway tunnel entrance.

9

- Fold a 3" strip of wet *Plaster Cloth* in half lengthwise, then widthwise.
- Dip in water and form cutaway tunnel using the shape of your hands as a guide.
- Test fit and shape to fit opening.

10

- Attach cutaway tunnel with wet strips of Plaster Cloth.
- Use a colored pencil (silver), draw ice block pattern on igloo.

11 Fig. 11a

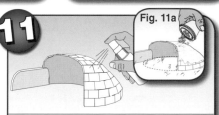

- ℹ️ **Project Glue in Spray Bottle** (pg. 170)
- Glue igloo to *Plaster Cloth* base.
- Spray diluted *Project Glue* on outside of igloo and on *Plaster Cloth* base.
- Sprinkle *Snowflakes* on wet glue. (Fig. 11a)
- Let dry.

12

- ℹ️ **Project Base & Backdrop** (pg. 95-96)
- Design a *Backdrop* that best fits your diorama.
- Cut off one side flap to use for Step 15.

13

- ℹ️ **Paint** (pg. 156-165) and **Backdrop Snow** (pg. 135)
- Paint *Backdrop*. Let dry.
- Spread Backdrop Snow on *Backdrop*.
- Sprinkle additional *Snowflakes* while mixture is wet. Let dry.

14

- Glue *Plaster Cloth* base and *Backdrop* to *Project Base*.
- Make sure the label area is facing foward.

15

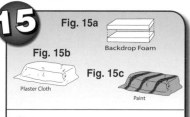
Fig. 15a
Backdrop Foam
Fig. 15b
Plaster Cloth
Fig. 15c
Paint

- ℹ️ **Sculpt** (pg. 138-145)
- Add realistic details.
- Sculpt a fire pit, pottery, etc. from modeling clay.
- Make a bed covered in a seal blanket (Fig. 15a, 15b and 15c).
- Make a sled from strips of cardstock. See our diorama!

16

- ℹ️ **Labels** (pg. 98-99)
- Label and add signage to your project.

AMAZON BASIN

Here's what we used...

SCENE**A**RAMA® Items

- **Water Diorama Kit**
- **Palm Trees**
- **Deciduous Trees**
- **Small Project Base and Backdrop**

Household Items

- Craft Paints and Brushes
- Cutting Surface
- Disposable Cups
- Hobby Knife
- Masking Tape
- Newspaper
- Pan for Water
- Pencil
- Scissors
- White Paper

Did you know?

The area known as the Amazon River Basin is fed by the Amazon River and its tributaries. The Amazon River begins in the Peruvian Andes, flows east 4,000 miles and empties into in the Atlantic Ocean. The Amazon River covers nine countries in South America: Brazil, Peru, Columbia, Guyana, French Guiana, Suriname, Bolivia, Venezuela and Ecuador.

Fun Fact!
More than half of the world's animal species live in the rainforests.

Highlands

Plains

Depressions

AMAZON BASIN

1

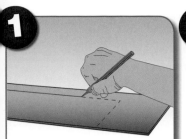

- Make a cardboard pad. Measure and cut a piece of cardboard *Side Panel* 10-3/8" x 7-1/8". You will build your diorama on this pad.

2

- Test fit *Backdrop* (in grooves) and cardboard pad on *Project Base*.
- Set aside *Project Base & Backdrop*.

3

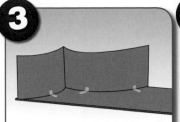

- Cut a separate strip of *Side Panel* (approx. 4" high and to desired length) to form front panel for higher terrain level.
- Arrange on cardboard pad in desired shape and tape in place.

4

- Cut additional *Side Panel* (approx. 2" high and to desired length) to form front panel for lower terrain level.
- Arrange on cardboard pad and tape in place.

5

- Cut a piece of *Side Panel* to fit level across back of terrain and tape to hold.

NOTE: *Side Panel* must NOT protrude over sides of cardboard pad.

6

ℹ️ **Newspaper Wads** (pg. 102)

- Use newspaper wads to fill terrain area.
- Keep terrain as flat and level as possible.

TIP! Place masking tape strips across top of terrain to help hold shape.

7

Fig. 7a

ℹ️ **Plaster Cloth** (pg. 104-105)

- Cover entire diorama with wet *Plaster Cloth* (3" strips), bumpy side up.
- Add 2 layers of *Plaster Cloth*.
- Overlap edges of cardboard by 1/2". (Fig. 7a)

NOTE: Holes in *Plaster Cloth* will let *Realistic Water* leak through to cardboard pad (Step 19).

8

- While *Plaster Cloth* is damp, test fit on *Project Base* with *Backdrop* in grooves.
- If it interferes with the *Backdrop*, make adjustments.
- Remove from *Project Base*.

9

Fig. 9a

- Roll pieces of wet *Plaster Cloth* into long, thin shapes.
- Lay on terrain to create edges of waterfall.
- Pinch wet *Plaster Cloth* to create a natural look. Let dry. (Fig. 9a)

10

ℹ️ **Waterfalls** (pg. 133)

- Spread *Water Effects* on *Release Paper* (slick side).
- Create waterfall in sections (will attach when dried).
- Feather ends with a tooth pick.
- Let dry until clear (approx. 24 hours).

11

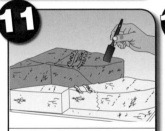

ℹ️ **Earth Undercoat** (pg. 171)

- Brush diluted *Earth Undercoat* over entire *Plaster Cloth* terrain.
- Let dry.

12

ℹ️ **Paint** (pg. 156-165)

- Use craft paints in natural colors to paint layers of Earth.
- Let dry.

TIP! Mix paint to create unique colors.

13

Fig. 13a

ℹ️ **Project Glue in Spray Bottle** (pg. 170)

- Spray diluted *Project Glue* on greenery areas.
- Sprinkle *Green Grass*. (Fig. 13a)

NOTE: Avoid spraying waterfall area, earth layers and depression.

14

ℹ️ **Foliage Fiber** (pg. 118)

- Stretch layers of *Foliage Fiber* until very thin and lacy.
- Lay over *Green Grass*, spray with *Project Glue*, then sprinkle *Forest Green Accents*.

15

- Apply *Project Glue* where you would like thicker sections of greenery.
- Press *Shrubs* into glue.
- Sprinkle *Evergreen Accent* on greenery to highlight landscape.

16

ℹ️ **Plant Trees** (pg. 128)

- Use a hobby knife to poke small holes in *Plaster Cloth* terrain to plant trees.
- Add a drop of *Project Glue* over hole and insert tree.
- Let dry.

17

Fig. 17a

- Spray entire landscaped area thoroughly with diluted *Project Glue* to seal.
- Let dry.
- Line edge of water area with a continuous bead of *Project Glue*. (Fig. 17a)

18

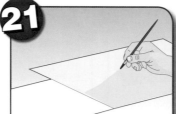

- Using white paper, create and color broad-leaf plants.
- Attach using *Project Glue*.

19

ℹ️ **Realistic Water** (pg. 130)
- Pour *Realistic Water* slowly on the depression area.
- Pull out to edges with the *Stir Stick*.
- Let dry until clear (approx. 24 hours).

20
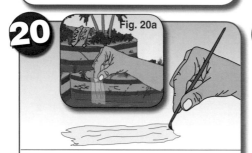
Fig. 20a

- Carefully peel dried *Water Effects* from *Release Paper*.
- Apply a small amount of *Water Effects* to the underside ends of waterfall.
- Press on desired locations. (Fig. 20a)
TIP! Dab *Water Effects* along base of waterfall.

21

ℹ️ **Project Base & Backdrop** (pg. 95-97)
- Design a *Backdrop* that best fits your diorama.
- Cut out with a hobby knife.
- Use craft paints or spray paint to paint your *Backdrop*.

22

ℹ️ **Labels** (pg. 98-99)
- Using *Project Glue*, attach *Backdrop* and diorama to *Base*.
- Make sure the label area faces forward.
- Label and add signage to your project.

Helpful Hint
We dabbed yellow paint on trees and bushes for subtle highlights.

More Ideas!
Let your imagination and creativity inspire you! Believe it or not, the same Scene-A-Rama products and modeling techniques used to construct the Amazon Basin diorama were used to build this Rainforest Ecosystem diorama. If you can imagine it, you can build it.

RAINFOREST ECOSYSTEM

ENVIRONMENTAL EFFECTS

Here's what we used...

SCENE A RAMA® Items

- **Water Diorama Kit**
- **Palm Trees**
- **Deciduous Trees**
- **Small Project Base and Backdrop**

Household Items

- Craft Paints and Brushes
- Cutting Surface
- Disposable Cup
- Hobby Knife
- Masking Tape
- Newspaper
- Pan for Water
- Pencil
- Scissors
- Small Sticks and Twigs

Did you know?

The largest rainforest in the world is the Amazon Rainforest. It plays an important role in stabilizing Earth's climate. How? Because of its size, it is able to absorb huge amounts of carbon dioxide and greenhouse gasses from the atmosphere. Deforestation is reducing the size of the Amazon Rainforest, resulting in devastating effects on our planet.

Fun Fact!

The Amazon Rainforest averages 9 feet of rain per year. About half is returned to the atmosphere through tree foliage.

1

- Make a cardboard pad. Measure and cut a piece of cardboard *Side Panel* 10-3/8" x 7-1/8". You will build your diorama on this pad.

2

- Test fit *Backdrop* (in grooves) and cardboard pad on *Project Base*.
- Set *Project Base & Backdrop* aside.

3

- ℹ️ **Newspaper Wads** (pg. 102)
- Arrange newspaper wads on cardboard pad to form terrain design.
- Tape to hold shape and hold in place.
- Newspaper wads must NOT protrude over sides of cardboard pad.

4

Fig. 4a

- ℹ️ **Plaster Cloth** (pg. 104-105)
- Cover diorama with wet *Plaster Cloth* (3" strips), bumpy side up.
- Add 2-3 layers of *Plaster Cloth*.
- Overlap edges of cardboard by 1/2". (Fig. 4a)
- **NOTE:** Holes in *Plaster Cloth* will let *Realistic Water* leak through to cardboard pad (Step 21).

5

- While *Plaster Cloth* is damp, test fit on *Project Base* with *Backdrop* in grooves.
- If it interferes with *Backdrop*, make adjustments.
- Remove from *Base*.

6

- Wad small pieces of wet *Plaster Cloth* into rock shapes.
- Place in desired locations along riverbed while *Plaster Cloth* is wet.

7

Fig. 7a

- Roll pieces of wet *Plaster Cloth* into long, thin shapes.
- Arrange on terrain to create edges for water runoff area.
- Pinch wet *Plaster Cloth* to create a natural look. (Fig. 7a)

8

Erosion

Riverbed

- Wad pieces of wet *Plaster Cloth* to create an erosion area along top edge of riverbed.
- Place on desired location while *Plaster Cloth* is wet.
- Pinch and shape *Plaster Cloth* to create a natural look.
- Let dry.

9

- ℹ️ **Earth Undercoat** (pg. 171)
- Brush diluted *Earth Undercoat* over entire *Plaster Cloth* terrain.
- Save remaining for Step 10.

10

- ℹ️ **Color Talus** (pg. 124)
- Pour *Talus* into remaining diluted *Earth Undercoat*.
- Mix with *Stir Stick*.
- Remove *Talus*, and let dry on newspaper.

11

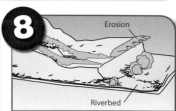

- ℹ️ **Paint Plaster Cloth Rocks** (pg. 116)
- Paint rocks.
- Dab paint in random patterns.
- Let dry.

12

Fig. 12a

- ℹ️ **Project Glue in Spray Bottle** (pg. 170)
- Spray diluted *Project Glue* on greenery areas.
- Sprinkle *Green Grass* on *Glue*. (Fig. 12a)
- Highlight with *Forest Green Accent*.
- Spray again to seal.

13

- ℹ️ **Foliage Fiber** (pg. 118)
- Stretch layers of *Foliage Fiber* until thin and lacy.
- Spray with diluted *Project Glue* and sprinkle with *Evergreen Accents*.
- Lay on diorama in preferred locations.
- Spray again with *Project Glue*.

14

Fig. 14a

- ℹ️ **Ground Cover** (pg. 116-125)
- Apply *Project Glue* where you would like shrubs.
- Press *Shrubs* into glue.
- Sprinkle *Evergreen Accent* to highlight landscape. (Fig. 14a)
- Spray with *Project Glue*.

15

- Cut *Deciduous Trees* into smaller trees.
- Cut trunks of *Palm Trees* to match height of *Deciduous Trees*, if desired.
- **TIP!** Cut branches at an angle for easier planting.

16

ℹ Plant Trees (pg. 128)

- Use a hobby knife to poke small holes in *Plaster Cloth* terrain to plant *Trees*.
- Add a drop of *Project Glue* over hole and insert *Tree*.
- Plant *Trees* one at a time working from the top, down.
- Let dry.

17

- Spray diluted *Project Glue* on desired rock debris areas.
- Sprinkle *Talus* on *Glue*.
- Spray additional diluted *Project Glue* on top of *Talus*.
- Let dry.

18

- Use twigs and natural items found outdoors to represent deforestation.
- Apply *Project Glue* where you would like fallen trees.
- Press twigs into *Project Glue*.
- Let dry.

19

- To seal, spray entire landscaped area thoroughly with diluted *Project Glue*.
- Let dry.

20

ℹ Water Effects (pg. 132)

- Dab *Water Effects* along runoff area.
- Let dry until clear (approx. 24 hours).

21

ℹ Realistic Water (pg. 130)

- Pour *Realistic Water* slowly over riverbed area.
- Let dry until clear (approx. 24 hours)

22

ℹ Project Base & Backdrop (pg. 95-97)

- Design a *Backdrop* that best fits your diorama. Let dry.
- Cut out with a hobby knife.
- Use craft paints to color your *Backdrop*.

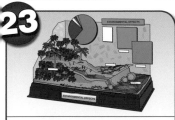

23

ℹ Labels (pg. 98-99)

- Using *Project Glue*, attach *Backdrop* and diorama to *Project Base*.
- Make sure the label area faces forward.
- Label and add signage to your project.

Fun Fact!

The Amazon Rainforest is the oldest rainforest in the world. It is estimated to be 100 million years old.

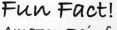

More Ideas!

Personalize your project with other easy-to-use Scene-A-Rama products and scenery materials. Sculpt animals that are indigenous to the rainforest and add them to your diorama. The Scene-A-Rama Sculpting Kit includes air-dry Sculpting Clay, Project Paints, sculpting tips and more. It's so easy to add creative elements to your rainforest diorama!

AFRICAN WILDLIFE

Here's what we used...

SCENE A RAMA® Items

- **Water Diorama Kit**
- **Scene Setters: African Wildlife**
- **Large Project Base & Backdrop**

Household Items

- Craft Paints and Brushes
- Cutting Surface
- Disposable Cups
- Hammer
- Hobby Knife
- Masking Tape
- Pan for Water
- Pencil
- Plastic Bag
- Ruler
- Scissors
- Sponge
- Tree-like Stick
- Twigs

Did you know?

Africa is home to vast amounts of diverse wildlife. People from all over the world travel to Africa to go on safari and view amazing creatures. Sadly, many African animals are listed as "endangered." Endangered animals are those that scientists feel are in imminent danger of becoming extinct.

Fun Fact!

A giraffe's tail is as long as its neck! In fact, it is longer if you add in the tassel of hair at the end.

1

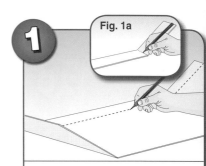

Fig. 1a

- Using a hobby knife, cut off a 3/4" strip along top edge of *Backdrop*.
- Cut off side flaps from 3/4" strip at folds. (Fig. 1a)
- This is the front panel for *Project Base*.

AFRICAN WILDLIFE

2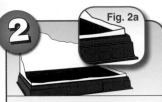

Fig. 2a

🛈 **Project Base & Backdrop** (pg. 93-95)

- Design a *Backdrop* that best fits your diorama.
- Make sure front strip and side flaps on *Backdrop* are level where they meet. (Fig. 2a)
- Test fit *Backdrop* and 3/4" front strip in grooves on *Project Base*.

3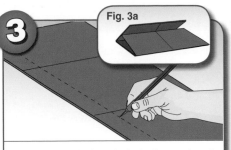

Fig. 3a

- Cut a 1" strip (lengthwise) off one edge of a *Side Panel*.
- Refold the *Side Panel*.
- Place both *Side Panels* side-by-side. Make sure the tri-folded edges are flush together and facing the same direction. (Fig. 3a)

4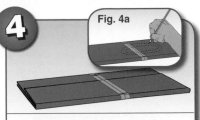

Fig. 4a

- Place masking tape around entire center seam of the *Side Panels* to attach them together and provide support.
- With the smooth side facing up, mark a bowl-shaped water area by drawing two irregularly shaped ovals, one inside the other. (Fig. 4a)

5

Fig. 5a

- Using a hobby knife, cut out larger oval from top layer of cardboard.
- Next, cut the smaller oval from middle layer, using cut out oval as a size guide.
- Bottom layer of cardboard should remain intact. (Fig. 5a)

6

- Test fit on *Project Base* with *Backdrop* in grooves.
- *Side Panels* should be approximately 1/8" smaller than *Project Base*.
- Remove *Side Panels* and set *Project Base* aside.

7

🛈 **Plaster Cloth** (pg. 104-105)

- Cover entire top of *Side Panels* with wet *Plaster Cloth* (3" strips), bumpy side up.
- Smooth *Plaster* bumps with wet fingers to fill holes in *Cloth*. Holes will let *Realistic Water* leak to cardboard (Step 15).
- While damp, test fit on *Project Base* with *Backdrop* in grooves.
- Overlap edges by 1/2".

8

🛈 **Earth Undercoat** (pg. 171)

- On dry *Plaster Cloth*, dab and brush diluted *Earth Undercoat* until covered.

NOTE: Save some diluted *Earth Undercoat* for Step 10.

9

🛈 **Paint Water Areas** (pg. 161)

- Paint center of water area with *Water Undercoat*.
- Dip *Foam Brush* in water and dab wet paint out to edges.

TIP! Darker paint in center of water area gives illusion of depth.

10

🛈 **Talus** (pg. 123-124)

- Crush *Talus*. A mixture of sand and larger *Talus* pieces gives the best effect.
- Pour crushed *Talus* into remaining *Earth Undercoat* and stir to mix.
- Remove *Talus*, and let dry on newspaper.

11

🛈 **Paint** (pg. 156-165)

- Use craft paints to paint *Backdrop* (front and back).
- Incorporate details such as a path, grasslands, trees, sky, etc.

TIP! We used a small piece of household sponge to paint trees.

12

- Using *Project Glue*, attach *Backdrop* and front strip to *Project Base*.
- Make sure the label area faces forward.
- Attach diorama to *Project Base* with *Project Glue*.

13

🛈 **Project Glue in Spray Bottle** (pg. 170)

- Spray diluted *Project Glue* on *Earth Undercoat*.
- Sprinkle *Talus* on desired areas.
- Spray again to seal.

NOTE: Avoid water area.

14

🛈 **Ground Cover** (pg. 116-125)

- Add *Foliage Fiber*.
- Add *Shrubs*.
- Add twigs for fallen branches.
- Add a tree-like twig for a tree.

15

🛈 **Realistic Water** (pg. 130)

- Pour half of the *Realistic Water* slowly in center of water area.
- Pull out to edges with *Stir Stick*. Let dry until clear.
- Then, pour remaining *Realistic Water*.

16

🛈 **Labels** (pg. 98-99)

- Use *Project Glue* to attach *Scene Setters* in desired areas.
- Label and add signage to your project.

NORTH AMERICAN WILDLIFE

Here's what we used...

SCENE**A**RAMA® Items

- **Mountain Diorama Kit**
- **Winter Effects**
- **Scene Setters: North American Wildlife**
- **Large Project Base & Backdrop**

Household Items

- Cutting Surface
- Disposable Cups
- Evergreen Clippings
- Glitter - Ultra-Fine Iridescent
- Hammer
- Hobby Knife
- Masking Tape
- Newspaper
- Pan for Water
- Plastic Bag
- Plastic Wrap
- Ruler
- Scissors

Did you know?

There are numerous zoos and national parks in North America where visitors can view animals in their natural habitats. A magnificent example is the United State's first national park, Yellowstone, with 2.2 million acres of wilderness and wonders.

Fun Fact!

Bear cubs learn about survival from their mother. She teaches them how to hunt, fish, climb trees and escape predators.

NORTH AMERICAN WILDLIFE

1

Rock Castings (pg. 108)
- Mix and use *Casting Plaster* per Basic Use instructions.
- Pour into *Rock Mold*, let set for 30-40 minutes.

TIP! For a variety of rock sizes, fill *Mold* less than half full and tilt on its edge.

2   Fig. 2a

- Using a hobby knife, cut off a 3/4" strip along top of *Backdrop*.
- Cut off side flaps from 3/4" strip at folds. (Fig. 2a)
- This is the front panel for *Project Base*.

3

Terrain Profile (pg. 105)
- Use the *Backdrop* to create the terrain profile for your diorama.
- Cut out using a hobby knife.

TIP! Find a photo of a wildlife scene to use as a reference for your diorama.

4

- Test fit *Backdrop* and 3/4" front strip in grooves on *Project Base*.
- Attach with *Project Glue*.
- Make sure the label area faces forward.

5

Newspaper Wads (pg. 102)
- Arrange newspaper wads into desired terrain shape over entire *Base*.
- Form a cave from smaller wads.
- Tape to hold in place.

6

Plaster Cloth (pg. 104-105)
- Cover newspaper wads with wet *Plaster Cloth* (3" strips), bumpy side up.
- Add 2 layers of *Plaster Cloth*.
- Turn diorama upside down and smooth wet *Plaster Cloth* on ceiling of cave.

7

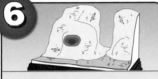

Attach and Blend Rocks (pg. 110)
- Attach Rock Castings to *Plaster Cloth* terrain.
- Poke 1" strips of wet *Plaster Cloth* around rock edges to fill in gaps.
- Let dry.

8

Leopard Spot (pg. 160)
- Dilute *Rock Colors*.
- Paint rocks with the Leopard Spot paint technique.

NOTE: Let rock castings dry 2-3 hours before coloring.

9

Earth Undercoat (pg. 171)
- Brush diluted *Earth Undercoat* over entire terrain (avoid rocks).
- Let dry.

NOTE: Save some diluted *Earth Undercoat* for Step 11.

10

Small Rocks & Sand (pg. 124)
- Pour *Talus* into a plastic bag and seal.
- On a safe surface, tap *Talus* with a hammer until desired size is achieved.

11

- Pour crushed *Talus* into remaining *Earth Undercoat*.
- Mix with *Stir Stick*.
- Remove *Talus*, and let dry on newpaper.

12

Project Glue in Spray Bottle (pg. 170) & **Ground Cover** (pg. 125)
- Spray diluted *Project Glue* on greenery areas.
- Sprinkle *Green Grass* on glue. Spray with additional diluted *Glue*.
- Lightly sprinkle *Evergreen Accent* to highlight. Spray with diluted *Glue*.
- Lightly sprinkle *Forest Green Accent* around rocks. Thoroughly spray with diluted *Glue* to seal.

13

Foliage Fiber (pg.118)
- Stretch a layer of *Foliage Fiber* until thin and lacy.
- Spray with diluted *Project Glue*.
- Sprinkle with *Accents*.
- Spray again to seal. Let dry.

14

- Glue sections of dried *Foliage Fiber* in place.
- Create vines and attach with *Project Glue*.
- Glue bunches of *Shrubs* in desired areas.

15

Evergreen Clippings (pg. 128)
- Spray evergreen clippings with diluted *Project Glue*.
- Sprinkle with desired color of *Accent*.
- Spray again to seal.

16

Plant Trees (pg.128-129)
- Plant trees in desired locations.
- Let dry.

TIP! Use twigs or dried flower clippings to model hibernating trees.

17

- Spray diluted *Project Glue* on rock debris areas.
- Sprinkle *Talus*.
- Spray again to seal.
- Let dry.

18

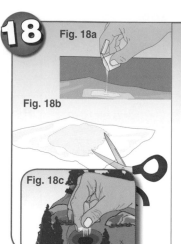

Fig. 18a

Fig. 18b

Fig. 18c

- Pour *Ice Effects* on a piece of plastic wrap and spread with *Stir Stick*. Let dry. (Fig. 18a)
- When dry, cut plastic wrap into icicle shapes. (Fig. 18b)
- Stretch and twist plastic wrap for more natural looking icicles.
- Attach to diorama with *Project Glue*. (Fig. 18c)

TIP! Sprinkle a small amount of ultra fine iridescent glitter on *Ice Effects* while it is wet. The glitter will make your icicles sparkle.

19

ℹ **Snow Mixture** (pg. 134)
- Mix equal amounts of *Snowflakes* and *Snow Base*.
- Apply mixture with Stir Stick on desired areas.
- Sprinkle *Snowflakes* on snow mixture (while still wet).

20

ℹ **Add Snow to Trees** (pg. 135)
- Using the *Stir Stick*, dab *Snow Mixture* on trees.
- Sprinkle additional *Snowflakes* while *Snow Mixture* is wet.

21

- Sprinkle *Snowflakes* over desired areas and spray with diluted *Project Glue* to seal.

22

ℹ **Labels** (pg. 98-99)
- Use *Project Glue* to attach *Scene Setters* in desired areas.
- Label and add signage to your project.

Helpful Hint
Create a summer scene by leaving off Winter Effects.

More Ideas!

Create the most unique project in the class! This amazing cave diorama was built with the same basic modeling techniques used in the North American Wildlife project. The stalactites are strips of Plaster Cloth coated with Casting Plaster. The stalagmites formed from Casting Plaster that dripped naturally from the stalactites, similar to how they are actually formed in nature.

CAVES

Here's what we used...

SCENEARAMA® Items

- **Mountain Diorama Kit**
- **Scene Setters: Prehistoric Life**
- **Large Project Base & Backdrop**

Household Items

- Clippings of Flowers and Bushes
- Craft Paints and Brushes
- Cutting Surface
- Disposable Cups
- Hobby Knife
- Masking Tape
- Measuring Spoons
- Newspaper
- Pan for Water
- Ruler
- Scissors
- Tree-like Twigs

Did you know?

Dinosaurs dominated Earth for more than 150 million years, making them some of the most enduring creatures to ever live. To date, more than 500 species of dinosaurs have been discovered. The word "dinosaur," which comes from Greek words meaning "terrible lizard," was created by Richard Owen in 1844.

Fun Fact!

The largest dinosaur eggs ever discovered are 1' long by 10" wide or about the size of a football.

PREHISTORIC LIFE

1

ℹ Rock Castings (pg. 108)
- Mix and use *Casting Plaster* per Basic Use instructions.
- Pour into *Rock Mold*, let set 30-40 minutes.

TIP! For a variety of rock sizes, fill *Mold* less than half full and tilt on its edge.

2 Fig. 2a

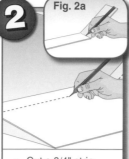

- Cut a 3/4" strip from top edge of *Backdrop*.
- Cut off side flaps from 3/4" strip at folds. (Fig. 2a)

3

ℹ Project Base & Backdrop (pg. 95-96)
- Design a *Backdrop* that best fits your diorama.
- Cut out using a hobby knife.
- Test fit *Backdrop* and 3/4" strip in grooves on *Project Base*.
- Make sure label area is facing forward.

4

ℹ Terrain Profile (pg. 105)
- Create a terrain profile from cardboard *Side Panels*.

5

- Form *Side Panels* inside of backdrop on *Project Base*.
- Tape in place to *Base* with masking tape.
- Remove *Backdrop* and set aside.

6

ℹ Newspaper Wads (pg. 102)
- Cover entire *Base* with newspaper wads. Arrange into desired terrain shape.
- Tape to hold in place.

7

ℹ Plaster Cloth (pg. 104-105) and **Edging** (pg. 106)
- Cover diorama with wet *Plaster Cloth* (3" strips), bumpy side up.
- Add 2 layers of *Plaster Cloth*.

NOTE: You will need to cut some 3" *Plaster Cloth* strips into 1" pieces (Step 8).

8

ℹ Attach and Blend Rocks (pg. 109-110)
- Attach rock castings to *Plaster Cloth* terrain.
- Poke 1" strips of wet *Plaster Cloth* around rock edges to fill in gaps.
- Let dry.

9

ℹ Leopard Spot (pg. 160)
- Dilute *Rock Colors*.
- Paint rocks with the Leopard Spot paint technique.

NOTE: Let rock castings dry 2-3 hours before coloring.

10

ℹ Earth Undercoat (pg. 171)
- Brush diluted *Earth Undercoat* over entire terrain (avoid rocks).
- Let dry.

NOTE: Save some diluted *Earth Undercoat* for Step 11.

11

ℹ Color Talus (pg. 124)
- Pour *Talus* into remaining *Earth Undercoat*.
- Mix with *Stir Stick*.
- Remove *Talus*, and let dry on newspaper.

12

ℹ Project Glue in Spray Bottle (pg. 170)
- Spray diluted *Project Glue* on desired greenery areas.
- Using *Plastic Cup* and *Sifter Lid*, sprinkle *Green Grass* on glue.

13

- Spray diluted *Project Glue* on *Talus* areas.
- Sprinkle *Talus*.
- Spray again to seal.
- Let dry.

14

ℹ Foliage Fiber (pg. 118)
- Separate *Foliage Fiber* into thin, lacy layers.
- Spray with diluted *Project Glue*.
- Sprinkle with *Evergreen* and *Forest Green Accents*, individually or as a mixture.

15

- Use diluted *Project Glue* to attach *Foliage Fiber*.
- Use *Foliage* for ground cover, moss, vines, tropical trees and more.

TIP! We dabbed craft paint on ground cover, *Shrubs* and *Foliage* to resemble flowers and new growth.

16

ℹ Deciduous Trees Using Natural Armatures (pg. 127)
- Prepare Puffy Tree Foliage.
- Apply a drop of *Project Glue* to tip of "branch" and press foliage into glue.
- Spray with diluted *Project Glue* to seal.

17
- Spray evergreen or flower clippings with diluted *Project Glue*.
- Sprinkle with desired color of *Accent*.
- Spray again to seal.

18
- *i* **Plant Trees** (pg. 128)
- Plant trees in desired locations.
- Let dry.

19
- Apply *Project Glue* where you would like bushes and fallen branches.
- Press *Shrubs*, prepared plant clippings and twigs into *Glue*.
- Spray with diluted *Project Glue* to seal.

20
- *i* **Paint** (pg. 156-165)
- Use craft paints to paint front and back of *Backdrop*.
- Let dry.

21
- To attach *Backdrop* to *Project Base*, use *Project Glue*.
- Glue front strip in place.

22
- Use *Project Glue* to attach *Scene Setters* in desired areas.

TIP! Attach the pteranodon to a piece of craft wire to resemble flight.

23
- *i* **Labels** (pg. 98-99)
- Label and add signage to your project.

Fun Fact!
Dinosaur fossils have been found on every continent in the world, including Antarctica!

Helpful Hint
Model plant life that reflects the climate of the Mesozoic era. During the Jurassic and Cretaceous periods, it was mostly tropical.

More Ideas!
Bring your project to life with Scene-A-Rama Scene Setters and ready-made Trees! Scene Setters are themed sets of people, animals and specialized items that are sized just right for dioramas and displays. With ready-made Trees, you can add a realistic effect to your project quickly and easily.

NATIVE AMERICAN HUNT

Here's what we used...

SCENE A RAMA® Items

- **Mountain Diorama Kit**
- **Scene Setters: Native American Hunt**
- **Large Project Base & Backdrop**

Household Items

- Craft Paints and Brushes
- Cutting Surface
- Disposable Cups
- Hobby Knife
- Measuring Spoons
- Newspaper
- Pan for Water
- Pencil
- Scissors
- Small Sticks and Tree-like Twigs

Did you know?

Native American tribes of the Great Plains Region hunted bison for survival. They used every part of the animal to make items like, food, clothing, tools, cooking utensils, pouches, containers, glue, fuel and jewelry. Before guns were adopted into their culture, Plains Indians killed bison with bows and arrows and spears.

Fun Fact!

Although bison appear large and lethargic, they are very agile creatures. They can run up to 35 mph and jump a 36" tall fence.

1

Rock Castings (pg. 108)

- Mix and use *Casting Plaster* per Basic Use instructions.
- Pour *Casting Plaster* into outside molds on *Rock Mold* tray until 1/2 full. Do NOT use inside mold.
- Repeat for a total of 6 rocks.

NATIVE AMERICAN HUNT

2

ℹ **Project Base & Backdrop**
(pg. 95-96)

- Design a *Backdrop* that best fits your diorama.
- Cut out using a hobby knife.

3

ℹ **Paint** (pg. 156-165)

- Paint a landscape design. Keep in mind that newspaper wads and *Plaster Cloth* will cover the bottom 1/3.
- Test fit on *Project Base* with label area facing forward.

4

- Arrange rock castings on edge along front of *Base*.
- When you have decided on your preferred configuration, note depth and height of rocks. You will use this information when arranging newspaper wads (Step 5).
- Set rock casting aside.

NOTE: Rock castings can be broken into smaller pieces.

5

ℹ **Newspaper Wads**
(pg. 102)

- Arrange newspaper wads into desired terrain shape. Wads should be approximate height of rock castings.
- Place wads far enough back on *Project Base* for rock castings to fit along the front.
- Tape to hold wads in place.

6

- Set *Backdrop* aside.
- Replace *Backdrop* with a temporary cardboard *Side Panel*.

7

ℹ **Plaster Cloth**
(pg. 104-105)

- Cover newspaper wads with wet *Plaster Cloth* (3" strips), bumpy side up.
- Smooth each strip with wet fingers to fill holes in *Cloth*.
- Add 2 layers of *Plaster Cloth*.

8

ℹ **Attach and Blend Rocks**
(pg. 109-110)

- Attach rock castings to front of *Plaster Cloth* terrain.
- Poke 1" strips of wet *Plaster Cloth* around rock edges to fill in gaps.
- Let dry.

9

ℹ **Leopard Spot**
(pg. 160)

- Dilute *Rock Colors* in *Mixing Tray*.
- Paint rocks with the Leopard Spot paint technique.

NOTE: Save some diluted *Rock Colors* for Step 11.

10

ℹ **Earth Undercoat**
(pg. 171)

- Brush diluted *Earth Undercoat* over entire terrain (avoid rocks).
- Let dry.

NOTE: Save some diluted *Earth Undercoat* for Step 11.

11

ℹ **Talus** (pg. 123-125)

- Pour some *Talus* into remaining *Rock Colors* and *Earth Undercoat*. This will give you a variety of natural rock colors.
- Mix with *Stir Stick*.
- Let *Talus* dry on newspaper.

12

ℹ **Project Glue in Spray Bottle** (pg. 170)

- Spray diluted *Project Glue* on desired greenery areas.
- Using *Plastic Cup* and *Sifter Lid*, sprinkle *Green Grass* on *Glue*.

13

ℹ **Ground Cover** (pg. 116-125)

- Sprinkle darker colors of *Accents* on *Green Grass* for realistic coloring.
- Apply *Project Glue* where you would like *Shrubs*. Press *Shrubs* into *Glue*.
- Spray again with diluted *Project Glue* to seal.

14

- Spray diluted *Project Glue* where you would like *Talus*.
- Sprinkle *Talus* and spray again with diluted *Project Glue* to seal.

TIP! Attach *Shrubs* to small twigs to create small bushes.

15

ℹ **Puffy Tree Foliage**
(pg. 119)

- Use *Foliage Fiber* to make Puffy Tree Foliage.
- Glue to landscape with *Project Glue*.

16

Fig. 16a

- Remove cardboard *Side Panel*.
- Glue twigs and other natural element in place.
- Attach *Scene Setters* and *Backdrop* with *Project Glue*. (Fig. 16a)

17

ℹ **Labels** (pg. 98-99)

- Paint outside of *Backdrop* black.
- Label and add signage to your project.

CLIFF DWELLINGS

Here's what we used...

SCENE A RAMA® Items

- **Mountain Diorama Kit**
- **Sculpting Kit**
- **Large Project Base & Backdrop**

Household Items

- Cutting Surface
- Disposable Cups
- Hobby Knife
- Masking Tape
- Measuring Spoons
- Newspaper
- Pan for Water
- Rolling Pin
- Ruler
- Scissors
- Small Sticks & Tree-like Twigs
- Wax Paper

Did you know?

Cliff dwellings are impressive, archaeological wonders built seven centuries ago in the shelter of canyon walls. They were constructed by a branch of the Pueblo Indians. Some cliff dwelling communities housed as many as 1,500 people. Most cliff dwellings are located in the Four Corners area where Arizona, New Mexico, Colorado and Utah meet.

Fun Fact!

The largest cliff dwelling in the United States is called Cliff Palace and is located in Mesa Verde National Park in southwest Colorado.

CLIFF DWELLINGS

36

Part 1: Create Cliff Dwelling Adobe Structure

1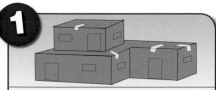

ℹ **Cliff Dwelling** (pg. 182-183)
- Use the Cliff Dwelling template to build your structure.
- Build a practice structure from a cardboard *Side Panel* before building clay dwelling. Make adjustments to template, if desired.

NOTE: Our dwelling is a two-story, three room structure, built with just the front and side walls and a roof.

2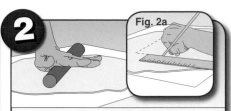

Fig. 2a

ℹ **Sculpt** (pg. 138-139)
- Flatten *Clay* (approx. 1/8" thick) with rolling pin between two sheets of wax paper.
- Following the template, cut out *Clay* using the *Sculpting Tool*. (Fig. 2a)
- To keep *Clay* fresh, store cutouts between sheets of wax paper or in a plastic bag.

3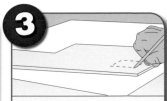

- Using the *Sculpting Tool*, cut openings in roofs for ladder.

NOTE: Our Cliff Dwelling was modeled after the Betatakin Ruin in Navajo County, AZ, where some earthen roofs and roof ladders are still intact after 700 years.

4

- Cut out windows and doors.
- Carefully remove cutouts for use in Step 5.

5

- Flatten door and window cutouts (1/16").
- Use the *Sculpting Tool* to add markings to resemble wooden boards.
- Add some light score marks to enhance wood look.

6

Fig. 6a

- Mark walls to create the look of adobe brick.
- Make notches along top of walls for roof beam supports. (Fig. 6a)
- Square walls with ruler.

7

- Measure width of door and window openings.
- Cut small sticks to fit over openings.
- Gently press into *Clay* and glue to hold.
- Let dry overnight.

8

- Paint window and door cutouts.
- Apply *Project Glue* around backside of window and door openings.
- Press window and door cutouts into glue (be sure decorative side is visible and straight).
- Let dry.

9

ℹ **Clay Structure** (pg. 143)
- Assemble walls with *Project Glue*.
- Let dry.

10

- Cut small twigs into 1/2" pieces (roof beam supports).
- Apply *Project Glue* in roof beam notches.
- Gently press sticks into notches.
- Let dry.

11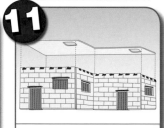

- Attach roof to first story with *Project Glue*.
- If roof is in two pieces, apply *Project Glue* where they meet.
- Let dry.

12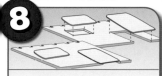

- Measure the height of the structure and cut out roof support posts from a *Side Panel* (used during building assembly in Step 13).
- 1" wide x height of structure, plus 1".

NOTE: Cut 4 supports for first story and cut 1 support for second story.

13

Back

- Fold a 1/2" lip on top and bottom.
- Attach roof supports to first story with *Project Glue*. Let dry.

14

Fig. 14a

- Glue second story to top of first story.
- Add roof support to back corner of second story. (Fig. 14a)
- Let dry.

NATIVE AMERICANS - *Cliff Dwellings*

37

15

- Cut sticks into desired lengths to make ladders.
- Assemble with *Project Glue*.
- Test fit ladders through roof openings on adobe dwelling.
- Set aside to dry.

16

ℹ️ **Paint** (pg. 156-165)
- Using *Project Paints*, finish painting the cliff dwelling.
- Set aside to dry.

TIP! Our dwelling was painted with diluted light tan paint (1-part paint to 1-part water). This allows the paint to seep into all the cracks and crevices. The doors and shutters were painted with slightly diluted brown.

Part 2: Create Cliff Dwelling Terrain

1

ℹ️ **Rock Castings** (pg. 108)
- Mix and use *Casting Plaster* as instructed.
- Pour into *Rock Mold*, let set for 30-40 minutes.
- To dislodge rocks, turn *Rock Mold* tray upside down and twist slightly.

2

Fig. 2a

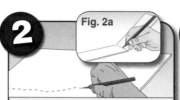

ℹ️ **Terrain Profile** (pg. 105)
- Using a hobby knife, cut a 2"-3" strip along top of *Backdrop*.
- Cut off side flaps from strips at folds. (Fig. 2a)
- This is front panel for *Project Base*.
- Draw terrain design on remaining *Backdrop* and cut it out.

3

- Attach *Backdrop* and front panel in grooves on *Project Base* using *Project Glue*.
- Tape to base for extra support.
- Make sure the label area is facing front.

4

ℹ️ **Newspaper Wads** (pg. 102)
- Arrange newspaper wads into desired terrain shape.
- Tape to hold shape of terrain.
- Leave flat area for adobe dwelling.

5

Fig. 5a

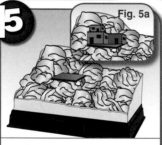

- Cut a section of *Side Panel* to form a landing for dwelling.
- Place in desired location.
- Test fit adobe dwelling with ladders. (Fig. 5a)
- Tape landing in place.

6

- Arrange newspaper wads into a cliff around location of dwelling.

7

ℹ️ **Plaster Cloth** (pg. 104-105) and **Edging** (pg. 106)
- Cover entire newspaper terrain with wet *Plaster Cloth* (3" strips), bumpy side up.
- Smooth each strip with wet fingers to fill holes in cloth.
- Apply 2 layers of *Plaster Cloth*.
- To plaster cloth difficult to reach areas, cut smaller strips of *Plaster Cloth*.
- Turn diorama upside down to plaster cloth ceiling of cliff.

8

Fig. 8a

ℹ️ **Attach and Blend Rocks** (pg. 109-110)
- Attach rocks to *Plaster Cloth* terrain.
- Press in place in desired locations.
- Poke 1" strips of wet *Plaster Cloth* around rock edges to fill in gaps. (Fig. 8a)
- Let dry.

9

ℹ️ **Leopard Spot** (pg. 160)
- Dilute *Rock Colors*.
- Paint rocks with the Leopard Spot paint technique.

NOTE: Save some diluted *Rock Colors* for Step 12.

10

ℹ️ **Earth Undercoat** (pg. 171)
- Brush diluted *Earth Undercoat* over entire terrain (avoid rocks).
- Let dry.

NOTE: Save some diluted *Earth Undercoat* for Step 12.

11

Project Glue in Spray Bottle (pg. 170) and Ground Cover (pg. 116-125)
- Spray diluted *Project Glue* on greenery areas (avoid rocks).
- Using *Plastic Cup and Sifter Lid*, sprinkle *Green Grass* on glue. Spray with diluted *Project Glue*.
- Lightly sprinkle *Evergreen Accent* to highlight.
- Lightly sprinkle *Forest Green Accent* around rocks.
- Spray additional *Project Glue* to seal.

12

Talus (pg. 123-125)
- Pour *Talus* into remaining *Earth Undercoat* and *Rock Colors*.
- Mix with *Stir Stick*.
- Remove *Talus*, and let dry on newspaper.

13
- Spray diluted *Project Glue* on desired "rock debris" areas.
- Sprinkle *Talus* on glue.
- Spray additional diluted *Project Glue* on top of Talus to adhere.
- Let dry.

14

Fig. 14a

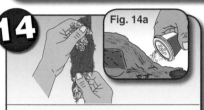

Foliage Fiber (pg. 118)
- Separate layers of *Foliage Fiber*.
- Stretch until very thin and lacy.
- Lay over greenery areas in preferred locations. Spray with diluted *Project Glue*.
- Sprinkle *Forest Green Accent* to highlight. (14a) Spray with diluted *Project Glue* to seal.

15

- Apply *Project Glue* where you would like *Shrubs*.
- Press *Shrubs* into glue.

16

Fig. 16a

Fig. 16b

Fig. 16c

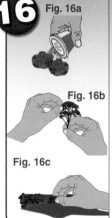

Natural Armatures (pg. 127) and Puffy Tree Foliage (pg. 119)
- Prepare Puffy Tree Foliage. Sprinkle with *Evergreen Accent*. (Fig. 16a)
- Apply *Project Glue* to "leaf" area of twig and press tree foliage into *Glue*. (Fig. 16b)
- Attach Puffy Tree Foliage to landscape for bushes. (Fig. 16c)

17

Plant Trees (pg. 128)
- Plant trees in desired locations.
- Let dry.

18
- Test fit cliff dwelling on diorama. If dwelling does not fit in opening properly, mark tight-fitting locations with a pencil.
- Using a hobby knife, cut into terrain, then press in with fingers.
- Test fit dwelling again. Repeat until dwelling has a nice fit.

19

- Attach cliff dwelling to diorama with *Project Glue*.
- Insert ladders and glue in place.

20

- To blend dwelling with terrain, apply *Project Glue* along base of dwelling and press in *Talus* and *Shrubs*.

21

Labels (pg. 98-99)
- Paint *Backdrop* material with black paint.
- Label and add signage to your project.

Helpful Hint
Use black acrylic or latex paint to paint the exterior Backdrop material.

TEPEE LIFE

Here's what we used...

SCENE A RAMA® Items

- **Building & Structure Kit**
- **Horizon & Detail Kit**
- **ShowBox**

Household Items

- Disposable Cups
- Pan for Water
- Sandpaper – Fine Grade
- Scissors

Did you know?

The tepee was first used by the Plains Indians of North America. Built from logs and animal hides, the tepee is an ideal nomadic dwelling for tribes that migrate often. Tepees are durable structures, strong enough to withstand wind, rain and heat.

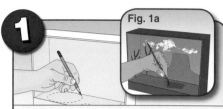

Fig. 1a

1

ℹ️ **Paint** (pg. 156-165)

- Assemble *ShowBox*.
- Use a pencil to sketch a Native American scene inside *ShowBox*.
- Mark location for tepee, mountains, river, fire pit, etc.
- Using *Project Paints*, paint Native American scene. (Fig. 1a)
- Let dry.

Fun Fact!

Native American family history was passed on through ceremonies, petroglyphs and pictographs.

2

ℹ Plaster Cloth (pg. 104-105)

- Add three-dimensional features to mountain landscape.
- Place *ShowBox* on its back. Cut a piece of *Plaster Cloth* and test fit over desired area.
- Dip *Cloth* in water, let some water drip off, then place on mountain terrain.
- Smooth to fill in holes, then pinch to add texture.

3

- Place additional pieces of *Plaster Cloth* on terrain for added texture and dimension.
- Let dry completely.

4

ℹ Paint (pg. 156-165)

- Paint *Plaster Cloth*.
- Paint lighter colors on raised areas and dark colors on flat areas. This will create shadows and depth.

5

ℹ Project Glue (pg. 170) & **Tree Foliage** (pg. 118)

- Use *Foliage Fiber* to make Tree Foliage.
- Use *Green Grass* for accent color.

6

- Apply *Project Glue* on leaf area of painted trees.
- Press small pieces of prepared Tree Foliage into glue.
- Repeat until satisfied with look of trees.

7

ℹ Native American Tepee Template (pg. 184)

- Glue Tepee template to *Project Cloth*.
- Unfold tepee flaps, then cut out tepee.
- Let dry.

NOTE: Create a door with excess *Project Cloth* glued to a small piece of *Project Stick*.

8

Fig. 8a

ℹ Paint (pg. 156-165)

- Paint tepee.
- When dry, form into tepee shape and glue together as indicated on template. (Fig. 8a)

TIP! For an aged look, brush with a color wash before painting designs.

9

ℹ Rinse Water (pg. 160)

- Use Lodge Pole Guide on Tepee template to measure length of *Project Sticks*. Cut with scissors.
- Use sandpaper to smooth or shape.
- Paint with a color wash.

10

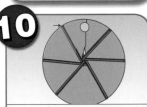

- Apply glue along bottom 2/3 of lodge poles, then insert through top of tepee. Line up poles with placement marks.
- Line up bottom of poles with bottom of tepee.
- Glue tepee in ShowBox.

11

Greenery

- Use prepared Tree Foliage to add ground cover.
- Attach with *Project Glue*.

12

River

- Place a piece of *Clear Plastic* over river area.
- Trace outline of river, then cut out with scissors.
- Attach with *Project Glue*.

13

Fig. 13a

Fire Pit

- Wad small pieces of wet *Plaster Cloth* into rock shapes.
- Let dry, then paint to resemble rocks. Glue into fire pit shape.
- Cut and shape *Project Sticks* for firewood. Dab on red and yellow paint to resemble fire. (Fig. 13a)

TIP! Use pebbles and twigs from outdoors.

14

Fig. 14a

Boulders and Smoke

- Wad pieces of wet *Plaster Cloth* into boulder shapes. Let dry, then paint.
- Remove a small piece of *White Fiber*. Pull thin and lacy. Paint gray, let dry, then glue to firewood. (Fig. 14a)

15

Fig. 15b

Fig. 15a

Fig. 15c

Tanning Rack

- Cut *Project Sticks*, then glue together in rack pattern. (Fig. 15a)
- Paint with thinned brown paint.
- Cut *Project Cloth* into an animal hide shape. Paint with a color wash. (Fig. 15b)
- Use *Project Wire* to attach hide to rack. Paint *Wire* brown. (Fig. 15c)
- Glue in place.

16

ℹ Native American Canoe Template (pg. 184)

- Use the Canoe template to make a canoe.
- Assemble and paint in desired colors.
- Glue in place.

TIP! Shape an oar from a *Project Stick*.

17

ℹ Labels (pg. 98-99)

- Paint outside of *ShowBox*, if desired.
- Label and add signage to your project.

HISTORY OF LOG CABINS

Here's what we used...

SCENE A RAMA® Items

- **Mountain Diorama Kit**
- **Ripplin' Water Kit**
- **Large Project Base & Backdrop**

Household Items

- Cardstock, 8" x 10"
- Craft Paints & Paintbrushes
- Cutting Surface
- Disposable Cups
- Hobby Knife
- Masking Tape
- Measuring Spoons
- Newspaper
- Pan for Water
- Ruler

Did you know?

Log Cabins have played a significant roll in the history of the United States. In the early part of the 19th century, the log cabin was a symbol of humble beginnings. The Whig party used the log cabin to show that 1840 presidential hopeful William Henry Harrison was a "man of the people." Harrison was elected the 9th President of the United States.

Fun Fact!

In 2009, the U.S. Mint distributed four newly designed one-cent pieces commemorating the 200th anniversary of Abraham Lincoln's birth. Each design depicts an era of Lincoln's life and career. The first release is the log cabin in Kentucky where Lincoln was born.

HISTORY OF LOG CABINS

1

Rock Castings
(pg.108)

- Mix and use *Casting Plaster* per Basic Use instructions.
- Pour into *Rock Mold*, let set for 30-40 minutes.
- To dislodge rocks, turn *Mold* upside down and twist slightly.

2

Fig. 2a
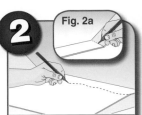

- Using a hobby knife, cut off a strip along top edge of *Backdrop*.
- Cut off side flaps from strip at folds. (Fig. 2a)
- This is the front panel for *Project Base*.

3

Terrain Profile (pg. 105)

- Cut out a terrain profile from *Backdrop* material.
- Attach terrain profile and front panel in grooves on *Project Base* with *Project Glue*.
- Make sure label area faces forward.

NOTE: Keep remaining *Backdrop* material to make the log cabin.

4

Log Cabin Template (pg. 178)

- Trace Log Cabin template on excess *Backdrop* material.
- Trace Chimney template on cardstock.
- Follow instructions on template.

5

Buildings & Structures
(pg. 147), **Drybrushing** (pg. 158) and **Paint Shingles** (pg. 162)

- Add Shingles to roof.
- Add a Stone Pattern to chimney.
- Assemble structure with *Project Glue*.
- Paint in desired colors and let dry. Weather cabin with the Drybrush paint technique.

6

Newspaper Wads (pg. 102)

- Arrange newspaper wads on *Project Base* into desired terrain design.
- Temporarily place log cabin in desired area to help form terrain.
- Tape newspaper wads to hold shape.
- Set log cabin aside.

7

Fig. 7a

Plaster Cloth (pg. 104-105) & Edging (pg. 106)

- Cover newspaper wads with wet *Plaster Cloth* (3" strips), bumpy side up.
- Smooth plaster with wet fingers to fill holes. Apply 2 layers of *Plaster Cloth*.
- *Plaster Cloth* should be smooth with edge of terrain. (Fig. 7a)

NOTE: Holes in *Plaster Cloth* will let *Realistic Water* leak through to base (Step 14).

8

Fig. 8a

Attach and Blend Rocks (pg. 109-110)

- Attach rocks to *Plaster Cloth* terrain.
- Poke 1" strips of wet *Plaster Cloth* around rock edges to fill in gaps. (Fig. 8a)
- Let dry.

NOTE: Be sure to leave room for the log cabin.

9

Leopard Spot
(pg. 160)

- Dilute *Rock Colors*.
- Paint rocks with the Leopard Spot paint technique.

10

Earth Undercoat
(pg. 171)

- Brush diluted *Earth Undercoat* over entire terrain (avoid rocks).
- Let dry.

11

Fig. 11a
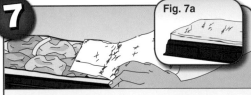

- Paint water area with *Water Undercoat*.
- Apply a continuous bead of *Project Glue* along pond outline. (Fig. 11a) Let dry.

12

Ground Cover
(pg. 116-125)

- Add ground cover to terrain. Let dry.
- Attach log cabin with *Project Glue*.
- Blend log cabin into terrain with *Shrubs* and *Talus*.
- Paint *Backdrop* material black.

13

Natural Armatures
(pg. 127)

- Make trees.
- Glue in place where desired.

14

Realistic Water
(pg. 130)

- Pour *Realistic Water* slowly on pond area.
- Pull out to edges with *Stir Stick*.
- Let dry until clear (approx. 24 hours).

15

Labels (pg. 98-99)

- Label and add signage to your project.

TIP! Make a dock from the cardboard *Side Panel*. Paint as desired.

BATTLE OF WILSON'S CREEK

Here's what we used...

SCENE·A·RAMA® Items

- **Mountain Diorama Kit**
- **Ripplin' Water Kit**
- **Deciduous Trees**
- **Scene Setters: American Civil War Soldiers**
- **Large Project Base & Backdrop**

Household Items

- Craft Paints and Brushes
- Cutting Surface
- Disposable Cups
- Hobby Knife
- Masking Tape
- Measuring Spoons
- Newspaper
- Pan for Water

Did you know?

The Battle of Wilson's Creek happened on August 10, 1861. It was the most significant Civil War battle west of the Mississippi River to date. A Confederate victory led to rebel control of southwestern Missouri.

Fun Fact!

At the beginning of the Civil War, Missouri declared themselves "armed neutral." They did not support the war efforts of the North or the South.

BATTLE OF WILSON'S CREEK, MISSOURI

1

ℹ **Rock Castings** (pg. 108)

- Mix and use *Casting Plaster* per Basic Use instructions.
- Pour into *Rock Mold*, let set for 30-40 min.
- To dislodge rocks, turn *Rock Mold* upside down and twist slightly.

2

- Use cardboard *Side Panels* to make a cardboard pad for the *Project Base*. The pad should measure 16" x 10 1/2".
- Use masking tape to attach cardboard pieces together.

3

- Test fit *Backdrop* (in grooves) and cardboard pad on *Project Base*.
- If cardboard pad interferes with *Backdrop*, make adjustments.

4

- Design a *Backdrop* and cut out with a hobby knife.
- Using a pencil, draw outline for mountain range on *Backdrop*.

5

ℹ **Newspaper Wads** (pg. 102)

- Arrange newspaper wads on cardboard pad inside mountain area.
- Tape in place. Do not tape to *Backdrop*.
- Remove cardboard pad and newspaper wads.

6

Fig. 6a

ℹ **Plaster Cloth** (pg. 104-105)

- Cover newspaper wads and cardboard pad with wet *Plaster Cloth* (3" strips), bumpy side up.
- Add 2 layers of *Plaster Cloth*.
- Overlap edges of cardboard pad by 1/2". (Fig. 6a)
- Test fit on *Project Base* with *Backdrops* in groves.

7

ℹ **Attach and Blend Rocks** (pg. 109-110)

- Attach rock castings to *Plaster Cloth* terrain.
- Poke 1" strips of wet *Plaster Cloth* around rock edges to fill in gaps.
- Let dry.

NOTE: Be careful not to drip glue or plaster on rock face.

8

- Using a pencil, draw your battle layout on *Plaster Cloth* base.
- Mark creek, burned out clearing, soldier locations, etc.

9

ℹ **Leopard Spot** (pg. 160)

- Dilute *Rock Colors*.
- Paint rocks with the Leopard Spot paint technique.

10

ℹ **Earth Undercoat** (pg. 171)

- Brush diluted *Earth Undercoat* over entire terrain (avoid rocks). Let dry.

NOTE: Save some diluted *Earth Undercoat* for Step 13.

11

Fig. 11a

- Paint creek with *Water Undercoat*.
- Apply a bead of *Project Glue* along creek outline. (Fig. 11a)
- Paint burned clearing.

12

ℹ **Ground Cover** (pg. 116-125)

- Spray diluted *Project Glue* on greenery areas (avoid rocks and creek).
- Apply landscape materials.

13

ℹ **Talus** (pg. 123-125)

- Color *Talus* in diluted *Earth Undercoat*.
- Apply *Project Glue* where you would like *Talus*.
- Press *Talus* into glue.

14

ℹ **Permanent Placement** (pg. 129)

- Permanently plant trees in desired locations.
- Let dry.

15

ℹ **Realistic Water** (pg. 130)

- Pour *Realistic Water* slowly on creek area.
- Pull out to edges with *Stir Stick*.
- Let dry until clear.

16

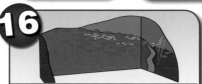

ℹ **Project Base & Backdrop** (pg. 95-97)

- Use craft paints to paint your *Backdrop*.
- Using *Project Glue*, attach *Backdrop* and diorama to *Project Base*.
- Make sure the label area faces forward.

TIP! On our diorama, the creek and mountain terrain extend to the painted *Backdrop*.

17

ℹ **Labels** (pg. 98-99)

- Label and add signage to your project.
- Attach *Scene Setters* using *Project Glue*.

EXPLORATION

Here's what we used...

SCENE A RAMA® Items

- **Building & Structure Kit**
- **Small Project Base & Backdrop**

Household Items

- Craft Paints and Brushes
- Cutting Surface
- Disposable Cup
- Hobby Knife
- Hole Punch
- Pencil
- Round Wood Toothpicks
- Twine

Did you know?

In preparation for the journey west, covered wagons were loaded with supplies needed for the long trip. The canvas-covered wagons were known as "prairie schooners," honoring their slight resemblance to white-sailed ships.

Helpful Hint!

Make sample Wagon and Ship from scrap paper. This is the best way to work out construction problems before hand.

1

Covered Wagon Template (pg. 187)
- Cut out the wagon pieces as indicated on Covered Wagon template.

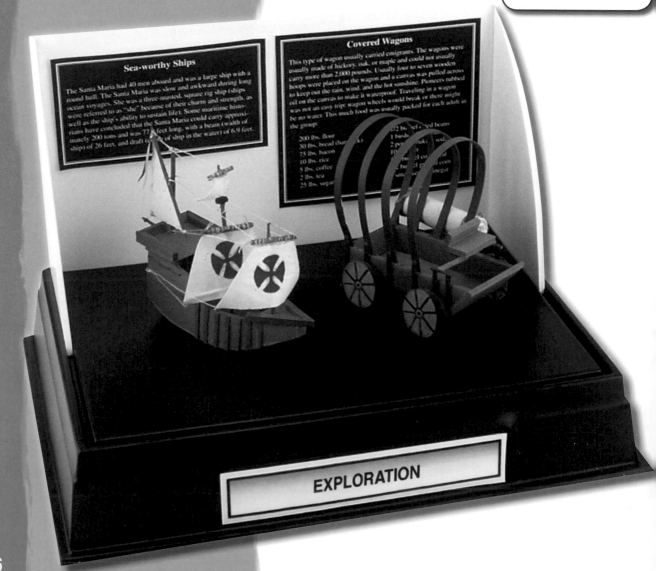

Sea-worthy Ships

The Santa Maria had 40 men aboard and was a large ship with a round hull. The Santa Maria was slow and awkward during long ocean voyages. She was a three-masted, square rig ship (ships were referred to as "she" because of their charm and strength, as well as the ship's ability to sustain human life). Some maritime historians have concluded that the Santa Maria could carry approximately 200 tons and was 77.5 feet long, with a beam (width of ship) of 26 feet, and draft (depth of ship in the water) of 6.9 feet.

Covered Wagons

This type of wagon usually carried emigrants. The wagons were usually made of hickory, oak, or maple and could not usually carry more than 2,000 pounds. Usually four to seven wooden hoops were placed on the wagon and a canvas was pulled across to keep out the rain, wind, and the hot sunshine. Pioneers rubbed oil on the canvas to make it waterproof. Traveling in a wagon was not an easy trip; wagon wheels would break or there might be no water. This much food was usually packed for each adult in the group:

200 lbs. flour
30 lbs. bread (hardtack)
75 lbs. bacon
10 lbs. rice
5 lbs. coffee
2 lbs. tea
25 lbs. sugar

EXPLORATION

46

2

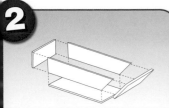

ℹ Contact Gluing Method (pg. 169)
- Use *Project Glue* and the Contact Gluing Method to glue wagon pieces A, B, C and D together as indicated on template.
- Let dry.

3

ℹ Paint (pg. 156)
- Paint wagon frame and remaining wagon pieces as desired.
- Let dry.

4

- When dry, run hoop strips through fingers to form a curve.

5

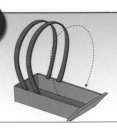

- Starting at the back of the wagon frame, push ends of strip into top edge of wagon sides (approx. 1/16" deep) and add a drop of glue to hold.
- Continue placing remaining strips, each 3/8" apart.

6

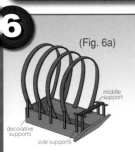

(Fig. 6a)

middle support

decorative supports

side supports

(Fig. 6b)

- Side Supports: From *Construction Board* cut two strips 1/4" x 3/4".
- Middle Support: From *Construction Board* cut one strip 3/8" x width of wagon. (Fig. 6a)
- Seat: Score seat cutout with a hobby knife, then gently fold up to create seat. (Fig. 6b)
- Using *Project Glue*, assemble seat and glue in place on wagon.
- Add decorative strips.

7

(Fig. 8a)

(Fig. 8b)

(Fig. 8c)

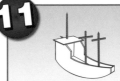

- Paint a wagon wheel pattern on each wheel cutout and let dry. (Fig. 7a)
- From *Project Sticks*, cut two 2-1/4" pieces for wheel axles. Paint and let dry. (Fig. 7b)
- Glue wheels to wheel axles (make sure wheel is centered).
- Glue wheel assemblies to underside of wagon. (Fig. 7c)

8

- Cut Project Cloth according to template. Fold in half lengthwise and roll.
- Using two small pieces of twine, tie to edge of wagon.

TIP! To cover the wagon, glue *Project Cloth* to wagon frame.

9

ℹ Exploration Ship Template (pg. 186)
- Cut out all ship pieces as indicated on template.
- Score sides of ship and ship railings as indicated with a hobby knife.

10

ℹ Contact Gluing Method (pg. 169)
- Apply *Project Glue* as indicated on template.
- Wait until glue becomes clear.
- Assemble as indicated on template.

11

- Cut a *Project Stick* 4" in length.
- Using sandpaper, sand stick round.
- Paint 4" *Project Stick* and 5 round toothpicks as desired and let dry.
- Using *Project Glue*, glue to ship as indicated on template

12

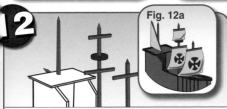

Fig. 12a

- Cut a 1" piece of round toothpick. Using a hole punch, cut a circle from *Project Board* for crow's nest.
- Paint ship, sails and above pieces as desired. Let dry.
- Using *Project Glue*, attach sails to ship. (Fig. 12a)
- Let dry.

13

- Pull threads from *Project Cloth* (or use sewing thread) to add sail lines.
- Attach around masts with *Project Glue*.

14

ℹ Labels (pg. 98-99)
- Attach wagon, ship and *Backdrop* to *Project Base*.
- Label and add informational signage to your project.

SANTA FE TRAIL PIONEERS

Here's what we used...

SCENE A RAMA Items

- **Desert Plants**
- **Desert Sand ReadyGrass Sheet**
- **Small Project Base & Backdrop**

Household Items

- Craft Paints & Brushes
- Cutting Surface
- Disposable Cups
- Eyedropper
- Hobby Knife
- Pebbles
- Figures

Did you know?

Opened in 1821, the Santa Fe Trail became the main commercial highway between Independence, Missouri and Santa Fe, New Mexico. Traders with freight wagons were a common sight along the Trail. Traders loaded two to three tons of goods into their wagons. At times the trail traversed several rivers, but most of the 900 miles were dry plains, deserts and mountains.

Fun Fact!

In 1880, the railroad reached Santa Fe, New Mexico replacing the Trail. Today, there remains approximately 200 miles of visible wagon ruts.

SANTA FE TRAIL PIONEERS

1

- Cut *ReadyGrass Sheet* in half widthwise.
- Test fit in *Project Base* with *Backdrop* in grooves.
- Trim *ReadyGrass Sheet*, if necessary.
- Set *Backdrop* aside.

2

- **ReadyGrass Sheets** (pg.114)
- Attach *ReadyGrass Sheet* per Basic Use instructions.
- Carefully align *ReadyGrass Sheet* on *Project Base* and press to adhere.

3

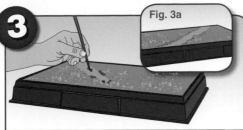

Fig. 3a

- **Project Glue** (pg. 170)
- To create wagon ruts, wet area with a paintbrush and water.
- Gently scrape *ReadyGrass Sheet* to rough up ruts. (Fig. 3a)
- Sprinkle pebbles along ruts and drizzle diluted *Project Glue* with eyedropper.

4

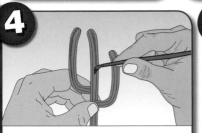

- **Paint Plants** (pg. 130)
- Paint *Desert Plants* with acrylic paint and let dry.
- When dry, attach to bases with *Project Glue*.

  TIP! If using tempra paint, mix in a tiny amount of glue.

5

- Dab *Cacti* tips with *Project Glue*, then dip in *Yellow* or *Red Flowers*.
- Let dry.

6

- **Foliage Fiber** (pg. 118)
- Separate *Foliage Fiber* into layers.
- Stretch until very thin and lacy.
- Break into desired size pieces.
- Attach to diorama with *Project Glue*.

7

- Using *Project Glue*, attach *Cacti*, freight wagon and figures in desired locations.

8

Fig. 8a

- Add tumbleweeds by rolling a small piece of *Foliage Fiber* into a small ball. Dab with brown paint.
- Attach to diorama with *Project Glue*.

  TIP! Use small pieces of *Foliage Fiber* sprinkled with *Yellow* or *Red Flowers* to hide bases of *Desert Plants*. They will blend naturally with the terrain. (Fig. 8a)

9

Fig. 9a   Fig. 9c

Fig. 9b

- Place a small amount of *Project Glue* on a piece of paper.
- Remove a pinch of *Wild Grass* and roll between fingers, creating an uneven look.
- Cut to desired length. (Fig. 9a)
- Dip cut end of *Wild Grass* in glue (Fig. 9b) and place on diorama in desired location. (Fig. 9c)

10

- Add natural elements from your yard. Attach with *Project Glue*.
- A pile of twigs could be a campfire.
- Clippings from bushes could resemble actual desert plants.

11

- **Project Base & Backdrop** (pg. 95-97)
- Use craft paints to paint your *Backdrop*.
- Attach to *Project Base* with *Project Glue*.

  TIP! Make sure the label area is facing forward.

12

- **Labels** (pg. 98-99)
- Label and add signage to your project.

  TIP! See Exploration diorama (pg. 46-47) for instructions to build a wagon.

THE ALAMO

Here's what we used...

SCENE A RAMA® Items

- **Basic Diorama Kit**
- **Building & Structure Kit**
- **Large Project Base & Backdrop**

Household Items

- Craft Paints and Brushes
- Cutting Surface
- Disposable Cup
- Hobby Knife
- Miniature Figures
- Pebbles
- Pencil
- Ruler
- Scissors

Did you know?

Originally named Missión San Antonio de Valero, the Alamo was built in 1724. The Alamo was home to missionaries and converts for nearly 70 years. San Antonio's five missions were secularized in 1793, and Spanish officials distributed the land to the remaining Native American residents.

Fun Fact!

Famous defenders of the Alamo included legendary Davy Crockett, famous frontiersman and Tennessee congressman.

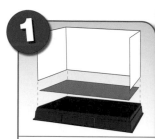

1

- Test fit *Backdrop* (in grooves) and *ReadyGrass Sheet* on *Project Base*.
- Trim *ReadyGrass Sheet*, if necessary.

THE ALAMO

50

2

ReadyGrass Sheets (pg. 114)
- Attach *ReadyGrass Sheet* per Basic Use instructions.
- Carefully align *ReadyGrass* on *Project Base* and press to adhere.

3

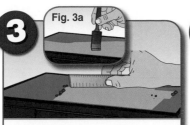
Fig. 3a

- Fill *Spray Bottle* with water.
- Spray *ReadyGrass* until damp.
- Scrape off grass with a ruler.
- Dip *Foam Brush* in water and brush scrape marks smooth, creating a "dusty" landscape. (Fig. 3a)

TIP! Keep grass for later use.

4

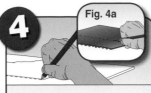
Fig. 4a

The Alamo Template (pg. 185)
- Copy Alamo Template. Cut out with scissors.
- Trace Alamo and archways templates on *Project Board*.
- Trace roof template on *Ribbed Board*. (Fig. 4a)
- Cut out with a hobby knife.

5

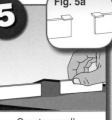
Fig. 5a

- Create a wall using *Project Board*.
- Add details to wall with additional pieces of *Project Board*. (Fig. 5a)

6

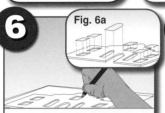
Fig. 6a

- Trace Alamo door and window cutouts on *Construction Board*.
- Paint windows and door on *Construction Board*.
- Cut out windows and door (slightly larger than drawn), then glue in place on back of Alamo. (Fig. 6a)

7

Brick Pattern (pg. 152)
- Using a pencil, draw a brick pattern on Alamo, archways and wall.

8

- Use *Project Board* and *Construction Board* to replicate the many unique details on the front of the Alamo.
- Cut out with a hobby knife.
- Attach using *Project Glue*.

NOTE: Use our diorama or a photo of the Alamo as a guide.

9

Paint (pg.156-165)
- Using craft paints, paint Alamo and archways.
- Let dry.

10

Assembly Techniques (pg. 154)
- Prepare walls for assembly.
- Use *Project Glue* to assemble Alamo.

11

Contact Gluing Method (pg. 169)
- Use *Project Gue* to attach Alamo, archways and brick walls to *Project Base*.

12

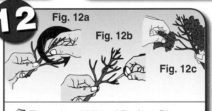
Fig. 12a
Fig. 12b
Fig. 12c

Trees (pg. 126) and **Project Glue** (pg. 170)
- Twist *Tree Armatures* into three-dimensional shapes. (Fig. 12a)
- Brush on *Sticky Bond*. (Fig. 12b)
- Allow to set until clear and tacky.
- Press *Shrubs* onto branches. (Fig. 12c)
- Spray tree with diluted *Project Glue*.

13

Ground Cover (pg. 116-125)
- Apply landscape materials per Basic Use instructions.
- Use pebbles or other items found in nature to add realism to your project.

14

Plant Trees (pg. 128)
- Plant trees in desired locations.
- Add landscape materials around trees as desired.
- Let dry.

15

Project Base & Backdrop (pg. 95-97)
- Design a *Backdrop* that best fits your diorama.
- Cut out using a hobby knife.
- Paint your *Backdrop* as desired.

16

Labels (pg. 98-99)
- Attach *Backdrop* to *Project Base* using *Project Glue*.
- Label and add signage to your project.

TIP! Add miniature figures to personalize your project

51

SAN DIEGO DE ALCALÁ

Here's what we used...

SCENE A RAMA® Items

- **Desert Oasis Kit**
- **Building & Structure Kit**
- **Small Project Base & Backdrop**

Household Items

- Craft Paints and Brushes
- Cutting Surface
- Disposable Cup
- Hobby Knife
- Pencil
- Ruler

Did you know?

The first of the 21 California missions was San Diego de Alcalá. It was founded in 1769 by Father Junípero Serra and named for St. Didacus of Alcalá. The mission got off to slow start, because the natives were leery of close contact with the missionaries.

Fun Fact!

Bells played a very important part in mission life. Most missions had a campanario (bell tower) to display their bells.

Helpful Hint

Research the mission of your choice thoroughly before you begin your project.

SAN DIEGO DE ALCALÁ MISSION

1

- Research the missions and print photos to use as a reference.

2

- Cut *ReadyGrass Sheet* in half widthhwise.
- Test fit *Project Base* with *Backdrop* in grooves.
- Trim *ReadyGrass Sheet*, if necessary.

3

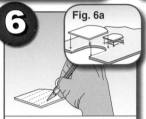

- ℹ **ReadyGrass Sheets** (pg. 114)
- Attach *ReadyGrass Sheet* per Basic Use instructions.
- Carefully align on *Project Base* and press to adhere.

4

- ℹ **Buildings & Structures** (pg. 147)
- Design mission structures.
- Using a pencil and a ruler, draw walls and bell tower on *Project Board*.
- Draw roof patterns on *Construction Board*.
- Cut out with a hobby knife.
- Test fit on *Project Base*.

5

- Place wall cutouts on a separate piece of *Project Board*. Trace window and door openings.
- Cut out windows and doors approx. 1/8" larger than trace lines.

6

Fig. 6a

- Score cutouts to create realistic wood textures.
- Paint as desired and let dry.
- Glue windows and doors to backside of walls. (Fig. 6a)

7

- Use pieces of *Project Board* and *Construction Board* to add details, such as crosses and ornate trim.
- Cut out with a hobby knife.
- Attach uslng *Project Glue*.

8

- ℹ **Paint** (pg. 156-165)
- Cut small pieces of *Project Sticks*.
- Paint with a brown color wash. Let dry.
- Glue in openings on bell tower.

TIP! Print a picture of bells and glue to *Project Sticks*.

9

- ℹ **Stone Pattern** (pg. 153) and **Color Wash** (pg. 158)
- Using *Construction Board*, create stone walkway.
- Draw stone pattern with a pencil.
- Paint walkway with a color wash. Let dry.
- Paint parts of mission if desired.

10

Fig. 10a

- ℹ **Assembly Techniques** (pg. 154)
- Prepare walls for assembly.
- Assemble walls, roofs and bell tower with *Project Glue* and let dry.
- Attach structures to brick walkway. (Fig. 10a)
- Let dry.

11

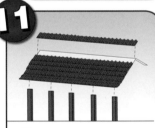

- ℹ **Spanish Tile Roof** (pg. 150)
- Use *Ribbcd Board* to add a Spanish Tile Roof.
- Add an awning using painted *Project Sticks* as wooden posts.

12

- Place mission assembly on *Project Base* and trace outline with a pencil on *ReadyGrass Sheet*.
- Note placement of buildings, paths, pond, etc.

13

- ℹ **Project Base & Backdrop** (pg. 95-96)
- With mission assembly on *Project Base*, design your Backdrop.
- Sketch scenery details with a pencil. Remove *Backdrop* and paint as desired.
- Let dry.
- Set mission assembly aside.

14

- ℹ **Remove Turf** (pg. 115)
- Remove *Desert Sand* turf for grassy areas, pond and placement of mission.

TIP! Save turf scrapings for a later use.

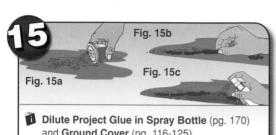

15

Fig. 15b
Fig. 15a
Fig. 15c

ℹ️ **Dilute Project Glue in Spray Bottle** (pg. 170) and **Ground Cover** (pg. 116-125)

• Spray diluted *Project Glue* where you would want grass. Sprinkle *Green Grass* on *Glue*. (Fig. 15a)

• Use *Foliage Fiber* to make hedges and bushes. Sprinkle with *Green Grass* or *Yellow Flowers*. (Fig. 15b)

• Use diluted *Project Glue* to attach *Talus* on path for added texture. (Fig. 15c)

16

Fig. 16a

• Paint pond. Let dry.

• Cut a piece of *Clear Plastic* to fit over pond. Attach with *Project Glue*. (Fig. 16a)

• Outline pond with larger pieces of *Talus*.

17

ℹ️ **Plant Trees** (pg. 128)

• Plant *Palm Trees* in desired locations.

• If desired, add additional landscape materials.

18

ℹ️ **Contact Gluing Method** (pg. 172)

• Attach *Backdrop* to *Project Base* using *Project Glue*.

• Glue mission assembly to *Project Base*.

19

ℹ️ **Labels** (pg. 98-99)

• Label and add signage to your project.

Helpful Hint

Flex Paste, available from Woodland Scenics, is great for adding a stucco texture to buildings.

A+

More Ideas!

Build any of the 21 California missions with Scene-A-Rama!

NUESTRA SEÑORA DE LA SOLEDAD MISSION
(Our Lady of the Solitude Mission)

SAN ANTONIO DE PADUA MISSION

SANTA BARBARA MISSION

LIFE ALONG THE NILE

Here's what we used...

SCENE·A·RAMA® Items

- **Desert Oasis Diorama Kit**
- **Ripplin' Water Kit**
- **Scene Setters: Egyptian Culture**
- **Large Project Base & Backdrop**

Household Items

- Corrugated Cardboard, 8" x 10"
- Craft Paints & Brushes
- CuttingSurface
- Disposable Cup
- Hobby Knife
- Invisible Tape
- Newspaper
- Scissors
- Muslin Fabric, 8" x 10"

Did you know?

Egyptian society thrived for 3000 years! The Egyptian's ability to use the Nile River was key to their cultural success. The Nile flooded every year, an event called inundation. The floods left behind a rich, black soil that was ideal for growing crops.

Fun Fact!

Recorded events show, when the Nile started to flood the clear water turned a murky red.

LIFE ALONG THE NILE

1

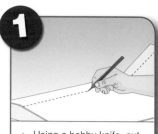

- Using a hobby knife, cut off a 7/8" strip along top edge of *Backdrop*. This is the front panel for *Project Base*.

2

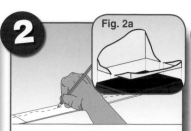

Fig. 2a

- Cut the side flaps of the front panel strip and *Backdrop* level with *Project Base*.
- *Backdrop* and front panel side flaps should set flush together. Test fit on *Project Base*. (Fig. 2a)
- See our diorama for ideas.

3

📄 **Paint** (pg. 156-165)

- Using craft paint, paint *Backdrop* and front panel. Let dry.
- Attach to *Project Base* with *Project Glue*.

NOTE: Make sure label area on *Project Base* faces forward.

4

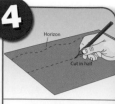

- Cut *Desert Sand ReadyGrass Sheet* in half lengthwise.
- On one half, draw and cut out a horizon along top edge.

5

- Apply *Project Glue* along top 1" of *ReadyGrass* (along horizon).
- Attach *ReadyGrass* at bottom 1/3 of *Backdrop*.
- Let dry.

6

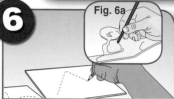

Fig. 6a

- Draw an Egyptian scene on excess *Backdrop* material.
- We chose the Sphinx and a pyramid.
- Cut out with a hobby knife.
- Score details on pyramid and Sphinx with hobby knife and handle of a paintbrush. (Fig. 6a)
- Paint as desired and let dry.

7

- Glue Egyptian scene to *Backdrop* partially covering *ReadyGrass*.

8

📄 **Egyptian Boat** (pg. 180) and **Paint** (pg. 156-165)

- Use the Egyptian Boat template and cardboard to create a boat for your diorama.
- Assemble as instructed on template page.
- Paint as desired.

9

Fig. 9a

- Wad small pieces of newspaper and place under *ReadyGrass*, up against *Backdrop* creating a small mound.
- Glue *ReadyGrass* in place over newspaper and to *Project Base*. (Fig. 9a)

10

- Glue second half of *ReadyGrass Sheet*, along front edge of front panel.
- Hold tightly in place until setting begins, then let dry.

11

Fig. 11a

- Wad small pieces of newspaper and place under *ReadyGrass*, creating another mound.
- Glue *ReadyGrass* to sides of front panel and *Project Base*. (Fig. 11a)
- Hold tightly in place until setting begins, then let dry.

12

- Test fit Egyptian boat on Nile area.
- Using a pencil, mark desired width of river on *ReadyGrass*.

13

📄 **Remove Turf** (pg. 115)

- Using the *Foam Brush*, brush water on *ReadyGrass* along area marked for Nile.
- Scrap off sand with handle of *Foam Brush*.

TIP! Save excess sand for a later use.

14

- Create the Nile River by brushing *Water Undercoat* on exposed area of *Project Base* and center edges of *ReadyGrass*.
- Let dry.

15

📄 **Project Glue in Spray Bottle** (pg. 170)

- Spray diluted *Project Glue* along river banks.
- Sprinkle *Desert Sand* scrapings and *Talus*.
- Spray again with *Project Glue* to seal.

16

📄 **Ground Cover** (pg. 116-125)

- Spray *Project Glue* on desired greenery areas.
- Sprinkle *Green Grass*, and spray again with *Project Glue* to seal.

17

ℹ Tree Foliage (pg. 118)

- Using *Foliage Fiber*, prepare *Tree Foliage*.
- Attach in desired locations with *Project Glue*.

18

ℹ Wild Grass (pg. 122)

- Attach *Wild Grass* in desired locations per Basic Use instructions.

19

ℹ Plant Trees (pg. 128)

- Bend *Palm Tree* trunks for a natural look.
- Plant in desired locations.

TIP! Change coloring of *Palms* with acrylic paint.

20

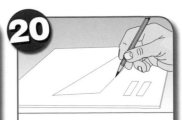

- Create a walkway using excess *Backdrop* material.
- Lightly score lines on walkway with a hobby knife.
- Paint as desired and let dry.

21

- Test fit walkway and boat in desired locations.
- Glue walkway at desired location.
- Let dry.

22

Fig. 22a

ℹ Realistic Water (pg. 130)

- Pour *Realistic Water* along area for Nile River.
- Pull out to edges with *Stir Stick* or tip of *Foam Brush*.
- Place boat on *Realistic Water*. (Fig. 22a)
- Let dry until clear (approx. 24 hours).
- Pour any remaining *Realistic Water* and let dry until clear.

23

- To create rolled rugs, cut small rectangles of white fabric.
- Pull threads from end of cloth to create a frayed look.
- Brush with *Project Glue* and roll up. Hold until setting begins.
- Let dry.

24

- Paint rugs with colorful colors.
- Let dry, then glue in place on boat.

25

ℹ Labels (pg. 98)

- Label and add signage to your project.
- Use *Project Glue* to attach *Scene Setters* in desired areas.

More Ideas!

The Egyptian Market diorama was made using techniques found in the Buildings & Structures in the Tips, Techniques & Templates sections. The project was enhanced with Scene-A-Rama Scene Setters and ready-made Palm Trees.

EGYPTIAN MARKET

DAILY LIFE IN ANCIENT EGYPT

Here's what we used...

SCENE-A-RAMA® Items

- **Desert Oasis Diorama Kit**
- **Building & Structure Kit**
- **Scene Setters: Egyptian Culture**
- **Small Project Base & Backdrop**

Household Items

- Craft Paints and Brushes
- Cutting Surface
- Disposable Cup
- Hobby Knife
- Scissors
- Sponge (small piece)

Did you know?

Most ancient Egyptia homes no longer exist. While massive stones were used for pyramids, homes were built with mudbricks. Over time, the mudbricks deteriorated and eventually crumbled away. Mudbricks were a mixture of mud, straw and pebbles. The mud mixture was poured into molds and dried in the sun for several days.

Fun Fact!

It was common for Egyptian villagers to spend a lot of time outdoors, including sleeping, cooking and eating on their flat-top roofs.

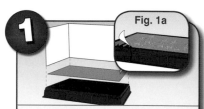

1

Fig. 1a

i **ReadyGrass Sheets** (pg. 114)

- Cut *ReadyGrass Sheet* in half widthwise.
- Test fit *Project Base* with *Backdrop* in grooves.
- Trim *ReadyGrass*, if necessary.
- Set *Backdrop* aside.
- Attach ReadyGrass per Basic Use instructions. (Fig. 1a)

DAILY LIFE IN ANCIENT EGYPT

2

ℹ️ **Buildings & Structures** (pg. 147)
- Design a structure for your diorama.
- Create a template from scrap paper and test fit on *Project Base*.

3

Fig. 3a
fold

- Trace wall and stair templates on *Ribbed Board*.
- Create front and side walls from a single piece of *Ribbed Board*. (Fig. 3a)
- Cut out with a hobby knife.

4

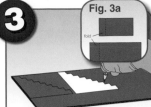

Fig. 4a

- Draw roof, windows and doors on *Project Board* and cut out with a hobby knife.
- Score lines on windows and doors lengthwise, with blunt end of a paintbrush. (Fig. 4a)

5

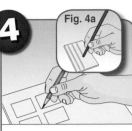

- Create rugs and awning fabric from *Project Cloth*.
- Pull a few threads from end of *Cloth* to create a frayed look.

6

Fig. 6a

Fig. 6b

Fig. 6c

ℹ️ **Paint** (pg. 156-165)
- Paint structure with craft paints. (Fig. 6a)
- Paint *Project Sticks* for stair steps, wood beams and awning poles. (Fig. 6b) Cut *Sticks* with a hobby knife.
- Paint rugs. Use a tiny piece of household sponge to paint flower design. (Fig. 6c)

7

Fig. 7a

- For each stair step, cut out two *Project Sticks* to desired length and glue side-by-side.
- Glue in place between two stair cutouts. (Fig. 7a)

8

- Using *Project Glue*, assemble structure.

NOTE: *Project Glue* dries clear and matte.

9

Fig. 9a

ℹ️ **Project Base & Backdrop** (pg. 95-96)
- Test fit structure on *Project Base* with *Backdrop* in groves.
- Trace around structure and set structure aside.
- Design a *Backdrop*. (Fig. 9a)
- Cut out *Backdrop* with a hobby knife.

10

ℹ️ **Paint** (pg. 156-165)
- Paint *Backdrop* with craft paints.

TIP! Incorporate leftover *ReadyGrass* in *Backdrop* design to create the illusion of depth.

11

Label

- Using *Project Glue*, attach *Backdrop* to *Project Base*.
- Glue structure in place.

NOTE: Make sure the label area is facing forward.

12

Fig. 12a

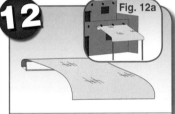

- Cut a strip of *Project Board* and glue to end of awning fabric.
- Glue to structure. (Fig. 12a)
- Attach awning poles (*Project Sticks*) with *Project Glue*.

13

- Glue rugs in desired locations.

TIP! For rolled rugs, use *Project Glue* to hold in place.

14

ℹ️ **Plant Trees** (pg. 128)
- Bend *Palm Tree* trunks for a natural look.
- Plant in desired locations.

TIP! To paint *Palms*, add a small amount of *Project Glue* to tempura paint or use acrylic paint.

15

ℹ️ **Diluted Mixtures** (pg. 170) and **Ground Cover** (pg. 116-125)
- Using included landscape materials, (*Foliage Fiber*, *Green Grass*, *Yellow Flowers*, *Talus* and *Wild Grass*), landscape diorama per Basic Use instructions.

16

EGYPTIAN MARKET

ℹ️ **Labels** (pg. 98-99)
- Label and add signage to your project.
- Use *Project Glue* to attach *Scene Setters*.

TIP! Personalize your diorama by adding unique details. We added a fountain!

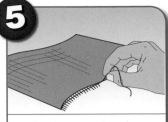

PYRAMIDS OF GIZA

Here's what we used...

SCENE A RAMA® Items

- **Desert Oasis Diorama Kit**
- **Plaster Cloth**
- **Small Project Base & Backdrop**

Household Items

- Cardstock, 8" x 10" (2)
- Craft Paints and Brushes
- Cutting Surface
- Disposable Cup
- Hobby Knife
- Scissors

Did you know?

The Great Pyramid of Giza, also known as The Pyramid of Khufu, was constructed around 2600 B.C. It is believed the ruling Egyptian pharaoh, Khufu (Cheops in Greek) wanted a grand tomb built for him that would last forever. For nearly 3,800 years it stood as the tallest man-made structure in the world, and more than 4,600 years later, it is still standing.

Fun Fact!

The Great Pyramid of Giza is one of the Seven Wonders of the Ancient World and the only one still in existence.

PYRAMIDS OF GIZA

1

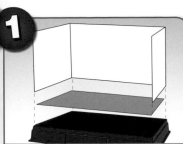

- Cut *ReadyGrass Sheet* in half widthwise.
- Test fit *Project Base* with *Backdrop* in grooves.
- Trim *ReadyGrass*, if necessary.
- Set Backdrop aside.

2

i **ReadyGrass Sheets** (pg. 114)
- Use *Sticky Bond* or *Project Glue* to attach *ReadyGrass Sheet*.
- Carefully align *ReadyGrass* on *Project Base* and press to adhere.

3

Fig. 3a

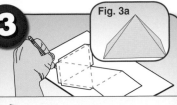

i **Pyramid Template** (pg. 173)
- Copy Pyramid template and trace on cardstock.
- Copy Pyramid template again for second pyramid, but reduce by 50%.
- Cut out, then fold and glue as indicated. (Fig. 3a)
- Let dry.

4

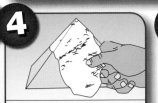

i **Plaster Cloth** (pg. 104-105)
- Cover pyramids with wet *Plaster Cloth* (3" strips), bumpy side up.
- Smooth each strip with wet fingers to fill holes in cloth.
- Let dry.

5

i **Paint** (pg. 156-165)
- Paint pyramids as desired.
- Let dry.

6

Fig. 6a

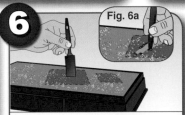

- Place pyramids on *Project Base*.
- Trace around pyramid bases.
- Wet area inside traced lines.
- Using *Foam Brush* handle, scrape *Sand* from inside traced area(s). (Fig. 6a)
- Save scrapings for Step 8.

7

i **Contact Gluing Method** (pg. 169)
- Using Project Glue, glue pyramids in place.
- Let dry.

8

Fig. 8a

Fig. 8b

i **Project Glue** (pg. 172)
- Sprinkle scraped *Desert Sand* around base of pyramids. (Fig. 8a)
- Spray with diluted *Project Glue*. (Fig. 8b)
- Let dry.

TIP! To create additional sand, crush *Talus* in a plastic bag and mix with *Desert Sand* scrapings.

9

i **Ground Cover** (pg. 116-125)
- Using the included landscape materials, add ground cover to diorama as desired.

10

Fig. 10a

i **Plant Trees** (pg. 128)
- Plant *Palm Trees* in desired locations.
- Cut *Palm Trees* to desired height. (Fig. 10a)
- Add landscape materials around *Trees* as desired.

11

i **Project Base & Backdrop** (pg. 95-97)
- Design a *Backdrop* that best fits your diorama.
- Cut out using a hobby knife.
- Paint your *Backdrop* as desired.

TIP! See our finished dioramas for ideas!

12

i **Labels** (pg. 98-99)
- Attach *Backdrop* to *Project Base* using *Project Glue*.
- Make sure the label area faces forward.
- Label, apply signage and add additional details to personalize your project.

Fun Fact!

Today, the tourist entrance to the Great Pyramid is a tunnel that was dug by grave robbers around AD 820.

PARTHENON

Here's what we used...

SCENE A RAMA Items

- **Plaster Cloth**
- **Desert Sand ReadyGrass Sheet**
- **Project Glue**
- **Small Project Base & Backdrop**

Household Items

- Cardstock, 8" x 10" (2)
- Craft Paints and Paintbrushes
- Cutting Surface
- Disposable Cup
- Drinking Straws (11)
- Foam Core Board, 8" x 10" (2)
- Hobby Knife
- Pan for Water
- Scissors

Did you know?

Located in Athens, Greece, the Parthenon is a temple dedicated to the Greek goddess Athena. The people of Greece considered Athena their protector. Built on the Athenian Acropolis, Parthenon construction was completed in 432 BC.

Fun Fact!

In 1897, a full-scale replica of the Parthenon was constructed for Tennessee's Centennial Exposition.

Today, it is a museum in Nashville's Centennial Park.

PARTHENON

1

- Cut *ReadyGrass Sheet* in half widthwise.
- Test fit *Project Base* with *Backdrop* in grooves.
- Trim *ReadyGrass*, if necessary.
- Set Backdrop aside.

2

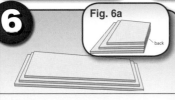

🛈 **ReadyGrass Sheets** (pg. 114)
- Use *Project Glue* to attach *ReadyGrass Sheet*.
- Carefully align *ReadyGrass* on *Project Base* and press to adhere.

3

🛈 **Plaster Cloth** (pg. 104-105)
- Create pillars by cutting straws to desired height (we made 11 straws, 2 3/4" H).
- Cut *Plaster Cloth* to height of straws.
- Roll wet *Plaster Cloth* around straws to desired thickness (3 or more layers).

4

- When *Plaster Cloth* is nearly dry, use a hobby knife to carve pillar design.
- Set aside until dry.

5

- Use a hobby knife to cut foam core board into squares, approx. 1/4" larger than top of each pillar.
- Use *Project Glue* to attach squares to pillars.
- Let dry.

6

Fig. 6a

back

🛈 **Contact Gluing Method** (pg. 169)
- Use foam core board to create entrance steps.
- Test fit pillars on foam board to determine size of top step.
- Back should be even. (Fig. 6a)
- Attach together with *Project Glue*.

7

- Use *Project Glue* to attach pillars to steps.
- Let dry.

NOTE: Place approx. 1" apart.

8

- Cut three strips of cardstock: one long front strip and two short side strips.
- Glue strips to top of pillars with *Project Glue*.

9

Fig. 9a

- For facade above pillars, cut equal size strips of foam core board (2 pcs, approx. 1/2" wide) and cardstock (1 pc).
- Repeat for left and right sides. (Fig. 9a)

10

- Glue one foam core board strip to top of pillars.
- Glue cardstock strip to top of foam core board.
- Glue second strip of foam core board to top of cardstock.
- Repeat for left and right sides.

11

Fig. 11a
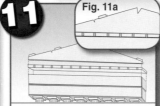

- Cut out roof and top facade from foam core board.
- Along edge of roof, make indentations with tip of a hobby knife. (Fig. 11a)
- Cut facade markings.
- Attach with *Project Glue*.

12

🛈 **Paint** (pg. 156-165)
- Paint Parthenon in desired color with craft paint.
- Paint a section of foam core board in same color (stones, Step 14).
- Let dry.

13

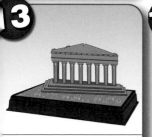

- Glue Parthenon to *Project Base*.

NOTE: Make sure label area on *Project Base* faces forward.

14

- Use a hobby knife to cut painted foam core board into stones.
- Attach to front of Parthenon with *Project Glue*.
- Touch up with paint as needed.

15

🛈 **Project Base & Backdrop** (pg. 95-96)
- Design a *Backdrop* that best fits your diorama.
- Cut out with a hobby knife.
- Paint *Backdrop* as desired, let dry and glue to *Project Base*.

16

🛈 **Labels** (pg. 98-99)
- Label and add signage to your project.

MEDIEVAL CASTLE

Here's what we used...

SCENE·A·RAMA® Items

- **Basic Diorama Kit**
- **Building & Structure Kit**
- **Ripplin' Water Kit**
- **Small Project Base & Backdrop**

Household Items

- Black Ultra Fine Point Permanent Marker
- Craft Paints and Brushes
- Cutting Surface
- Disposable Cup
- Flat Wood Toothpicks
- Hobby Knife
- Pencil
- Rubber Bands
- Ruler
- Scissors
- White Paper

Did you know?

Medieval castles were built more for protection than comfort. They are among the most secure buildings ever constructed. Building these military defenses eventually grew into a competition between lords to construct the most magnificent structures in the world.

Fun Fact!

It was the job of the knights to defend the castle and protect the lord and lady whom they served.

CASTLE PROJECT

1

- Cut *ReadyGrass Sheet* in half widthwise.
- Test fit *Project Base* with *Backdrop* in grooves.
- Trim *ReadyGrass*, if necessary.
- Set Backdrop aside.

2

📋 ReadyGrass Sheets (pg. 114)
- Attach *ReadyGrass Sheet* per Basic Use instructions.
- Align *ReadyGrass* on *Project Base* and press to adhere.

3

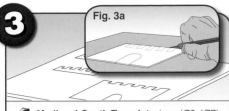
Fig. 3a

📋 Medieval CastleTemplate (pg. 176-177)
- Trace Medieval Castle Front (1x) on *Project Board*.
- Trace Tower (2x), Spire (2x), Parapet (2x) and Disk (2x) on *Construction Board*.
- Using a hobby knife, cut out all castle pieces (except the castle door, windows and crenellation). (Fig. 3a)

4

📋 Brick Pattern (pg. 152)
- Using a black, ultra fine point permanent marker and a ruler, draw brick pattern on castle front wall, towers and parapets.

TIP! Our brickwork pattern was drawn with a height of 1/8".

5

- Using a hobby knife, cut out castle door and crenellation.
- Save castle door cutout for Step 15.

6

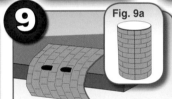

- Paint backside of front wall and parapet with black craft paint.
- Paint all visible edges with black paint.
- Let dry.

7

Fig. 7a

📋 Paint (pg. 156-165)
- Paint castle pieces in desired colors.
- Paint windows on front wall and towers with black paint. (Fig. 7a) Let dry.

TIP! Our Medieval Castle was painted with the Stippling paint technique.

8

Fig. 8a

- Form cones into spire shape and tape inside to hold.
- Apply *Project Glue* along outside seams.
- Smooth glue to seal any gaps.
- Glue to disks. (Fig. 8a)

9

Fig. 9a

- Run tower cutouts along a table edge to curve.
- Roll together forming a circle (1 1/4" in diameter). Tape inside to hold.
- Apply *Project Glue* along outside seams. (Fig. 9a)

TIP! Hold with rubber bands while drying.

10

Fig. 10a

- Run parapets along a table edge to curve.
- Form into circles to fit spires and tape to hold (tape inside parapet). (Fig. 10a)
- Apply *Project Glue* along outside seam.
- Let dry.

11

- Using *Construction Board*, cut out two flags.
- Paint desired colors.
- Glue a piece of *Project Wire* to each flag, and glue to spires.

12

- Using *Project Glue*, glue each parapet to a spire.
- Let dry.

TIP! Align seams of parapet and spire.

13

- Align tower and parapet seams.
- Glue parapet assembly to tower.
- Let dry.

14

- Glue towers to front wall.
- Let dry.

15

Fig. 15a

Create Portcullis (Castle Gate)
NOTE: Use castle door cutout as a template.
- Lay five flat toothpicks side-by-side with pointed ends facing same direction.
- Glue four 1 1/2" toothpick pieces across sections. (Fig. 15a)
- Paint desired color.
- Glue portcullis to backside of front wall.

16 — Create Drawbridge

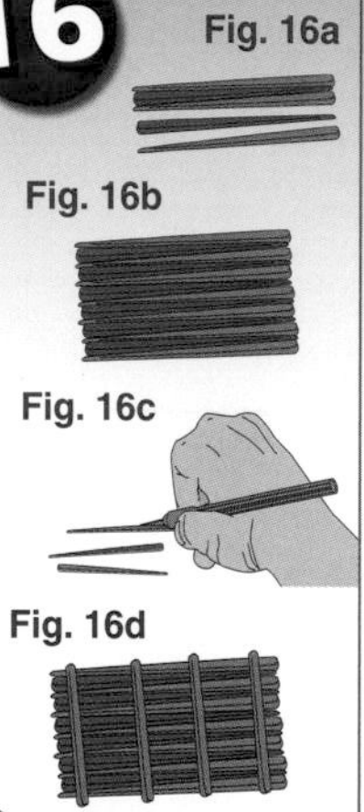

Fig. 16a

Fig. 16b

Fig. 16c

Fig. 16d

- Lay flat toothpicks side-by-side, alternating direction (approx. 22 ea, 1 3/8" in length). (Fig. 16a)
- Glue together and let dry. (Fig. 16b)
- Cut four toothpicks to a length of 1 1/2" for cross-section pieces. (Fig. 16c)
- Glue cross-section pieces in place. Let dry. (Fig. 16d)
- Paint desired color.

17

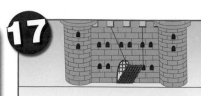

- Glue base of drawbridge to bottom of castle entrance.
- Cut two pieces of *Project Wire* for drawbridge chain.
- Attach one end of wire to crenellation and opposite end to drawbridge.
- Paint black lines on wire for a chainlike look.

TIP! See our finished diorama for ideas!

18

- Set assembled castle on *Project Base* with label area facing forward.
- Using a pencil, draw castle grounds moat, garden, bailey, well, etc.
- Set assembled castle aside.

19

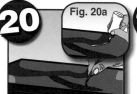

- To remove *ReadyGrass* (for moat, garden, etc), wet outlined areas with water.
- Scrape off grass carefully.

NOTE: Save loose grass for later use.

20

Fig. 20a

Paint (pg. 156-165)
- Paint roads, paths, moat and garden area.
- Line outer edges of moat area with a continuous bead of *Project Glue*. (Fig. 20a)
- Let dry for 1 hour.

21

- Glue castle to *ReadyGrass Sheet*.
- Let dry.

22

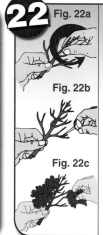
Fig. 22a

Fig. 22b

Fig. 22c

Project Glue in Spray Bottle (pg. 170) and **Trees** (pg. 126)
- Twist *Tree Armatures* into three-dimensional shapes. (Fig. 22a)
- Brush *Sticky Bond* on "leaf" area of branches. Wait until clear and tacky. (Fig. 22b)
- Firmly press *Shrubs/Foliage* onto branches. (Fig. 22c)
- Sprinkle lightly with *Yellow Flowers*.
- Spray tree with diluted *Project Glue* to seal.

23

Plant Trees (pg. 128)
- Using the tip of hobby knife, poke hole through *ReadyGrass Sheet* into *Project Base*.
- Cover hole with a drop of *Project Glue*.
- Place tree in hole.
- Let dry.

24

Ground Cover (pg. 116-125)
- Apply *Project Glue* where you would like bushes and garden plants.
- Press *Shrubs/Foliage* into glue.
- Highlight with *Yellow Flowers* and/or *Accents*.
- Spray with diluted *Project Glue* to seal.

25

Realistic Water (pg. 130)
- Slowly pour *Realistic Water* on moat area.
- Pull out to edges with *Stir Stick*.
- Let dry until clear (approx. 24 hours).

26

Fig. 26a

Fig. 26b

Fig. 26c

Fig. 26d

Fig. 26e

Buildings & Structures (pg. 147)
- Use flat toothpicks, *Project Board*, *Project Sticks*, *Construction Board* and other household items to add details.

Examples: Wooden Cart (Fig. 26a), Wooden Shutters (Fig. 26b), Wood Pile (Fig. 26c), Crest Markers (Fig. 26d), Farmhouse with *Wild Grass* roof (Fig. 26e).

27

Project Base & Backdrop (pg. 95-96)
- Design a *Backdrop* that best fits your diorama.
- Cut out using a hobby knife.
- Use craft paints to paint your *Backdrop*.

28

Labels (pg. 98-99)
- Attach *Backdrop* to *Project Base* using *Project Glue*.
- Label and add signage to your project.

BURG ELTZ

Here's what we used...

SCENEARAMA® Items

- **Water Diorama Kit**
- **Deciduous Trees**
- **Small Project Base & Backdrop**

Household Items

- Cardstock, 8" x 10"
- Craft Paints and Brushes
- Cutting Surface
- Disposable Cup
- Foam Core Board, 8" x 10" (2)
- Hobby Knife
- Miniature Horseman Figure
- Pencil
- Rubber Bands
- Ruler
- Scissors
- White Paper

Did you know?

In true German tradition, Eltz Castle was built as a fortified residence. It was not designed to be, nor ever used as, a military post. As such, it was not damaged or destroyed in battle and its original features remain intact today. Earliest Date: 1157. Earliest Family Name: Rudolf von Eltz.

Fun Fact!

Eltz Castle has remained in the possession of the Eltz family for more than 800 years.

BURG ELTZ

1

- Make a cardboard pad. Measure and cut a cardboard *Side Panel* 10 3/8" x 7 1/8". You will build your diorama on this cardboard pad.

2

- Test fit *Backdrop* (in grooves) and cardboard pad on *Project Base*.

3

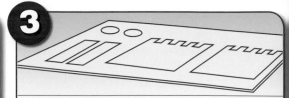

📘 Buildings and Structures (pg. 147-155)

- On white paper, design and cut out your castle. Keep in mind the size of the *Project Base*, *Backdrop* and terrain.
- Trace castle sections on foam board or cardstock.
- Cut out castle sections with a hobby knife.

TIP! We used cardstock to construct towers and spires, and foam board for main structure and bridge.

4

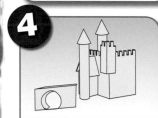

- Using *Project Glue*, assemble and glue castle and bridge.

NOTE: It may be easier to glue certain pieces together after terrain is complete.

5

- Test fit castle and bridge on *Project Base* with *Backdrop* in grooves.
- Trace outline of bridge and castle placement on cardboard pad.

6

📘 Newspaper Wads (pg. 102)

- Arrange and tape newspaper wads into a mountain shape on cardboard pad.
- Test fit on *Project Base* with castle, bridge and *Backdrop*.
- If needed, make adjustments to wads for castle, bridge and *Backdrop*.
- Remove castle and bridge.

7

- Finish taping newspaper wads to cardboard to hold shape.
- Newspaper wads must NOT protrude over sides of cardboard.

8

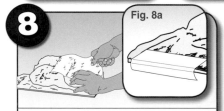
Fig. 8a

📘 Plaster Cloth (pg. 104-105)

- Cover newspaper and cardboard with wet *Plaster Cloth* (3" strips), bumpy side up.
- Add 2 layers of *Plaster Cloth*.
- Overlap edges of cardboard by 1/2". (Fig. 8a)

9

- While *Plaster Cloth* is damp, test fit on *Project Base* with *Backdrop* in grooves.
- If it interferes with *Backdrop*, make adjustments.
- Test fit castle and bridge.
- Remove from *Project Base*.
- Let dry.

10

Fig. 10a

📘 Paint (pg. 156-165)

- Paint castle in desired colors.
- Draw windows with a pencil then paint with black paint. (Fig. 10a)
- Let dry.

TIP! After our Castle was painted, we aged it with the Drybrushing paint technique.

11

📘 Earth Undercoat (pg. 171)

- Using the *Foam Brush*, paint entire *Plaster Cloth* surface with diluted *Earth Undercoat*. Let dry.
- Paint water area with *Water Undercoat*, if desired.
- Let dry.

NOTE: Save some diluted *Earth Undercoat* for Step 15.

12

📘 Project Glue in Spray Bottle (pg. 170)

- Spray diluted *Project Glue* over entire *Plaster Cloth* mountain. Avoid water area.
- Sprinkle *Green Grass* on glue.
- Shake off excess. Save for later use.

13

📘 Foliage Fiber (pg. 118)

- Separate layers of *Foliage Fiber* and stretch until thin and lacy.
- Lay over *Green Grass*.
- Spray with diluted *Project Glue* and sprinkle with *Accents*.

14

ⓘ Ground Cover (pg. 114-125)

- Apply *Project Glue* where you would like thicker sections of greenery, then press *Shrubs* into *Glue*.
- Spray *Shrubs* with diluted *Project Glue*, sprinkle *Evergreen* and *Forest Green Accents* to highlight landscape and spray again to seal.

15

ⓘ Talus (pg. 123-125)

- Color *Talus* with diluted *Earth Undercoat*. Let dry.
- Spray diluted *Project Glue* around mountain base, sprinkle on *Talus* and spray again.

16

- Attach castle to mountain using *Project Glue*.
- You may need to make adjustments to castle base to get it to fit properly.
- Hide gaps between castle and terrain with ground cover materials.

17

- Using scissors, cut *Deciduous Trees* into smaller trees and bushes.
- Trees and bushes should be appropriate to size of castle.

NOTE: Cut branches at an angle for easier planting.

18

ⓘ Plant Trees (pg. 128)

- Use a hobby knife to poke small holes in *Plaster Cloth* terrain to plant trees.
- Plant one tree at a time, working from the back, forward.
- Add a drop of *Project Glue* over hole, and insert *Tree*. Let dry.

19

- Apply a continuous bead of *Project Glue* around edge of water area.
- Let dry for 1 hour.

20

ⓘ Backdrop (pg. 95-96)

- Design a *Backdrop* that best fits your diorama.
- Cut out using a hobby knife.
- Paint your *Backdrop* as desired.

TIP! See our dioramas for ideas!

21

- Brush diluted *Project Glue* on *Backdrop* behind castle bridge.
- Sprinkle desired *Accent* color to represent grass.
- Shake off excess.

22

- Using *Project Glue*, attach *Backdrop* and diorama to *Project Base*.
- Make sure the label area faces forward.
- Using *Project Glue*, glue castle and bridge in place.

23

ⓘ Realistic Water (pg. 130)

- Pour *Realistic Water* slowly on water area.
- Brush out to edges with *Stir Stick*.
- Let dry completely (approx 24 hours).
- When dry, add any remaining *Realistic Water*.

24

ⓘ Labels (pg. 98-99)

- Label and add signage to your project.

TIP! Add miniature horseman and other details to your project.

More Ideas!

Here is a Castle project done by our testing student Jaqui. Currently, the project is proudly displayed on a bedroom shelve.

CASTLE LIFE

Here's what we used...

SCENE A RAMA Items

- Foliage & Grasses
- Ripplin' Water Kit
- Green Grass ReadyGrass Sheet
- Small Project Base & Backdrop

Household Items

- Cardstock 8" x 10"
- Craft Paints and Brushes
- Craft Wire
- Cutting Mat
- Disposable Cup
- Hobby Knife
- Metal Ruler
- Miniature Farm Animals
- Pebbles
- Pencil
- Scissors
- Toothpicks - Flat & Round, Wood

Did you know?

A castle built in the Middle Ages was more than a home, it was also a fortress. To guard against attacks, most castles were surrounded by two stone walls. The walls acted as a double line of defense.

CASTLE LIFE

1

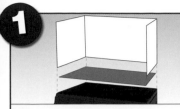

ℹ **Attach ReadyGrass** (pg. 114-115)
- Cut *ReadyGrass Sheet* in half widthwise.
- Test fit *Project Base* with *Backdrop* in grooves.
- Trim *ReadyGrass*, if necessary.
- Set Backdrop aside.
- Attach per Basic Use instructions.

2

- The castle is formed from *Backdrop* material. This creates a unique, three-dimensional structure.
- New fold lines will need to be made, and the original may not be used.

3

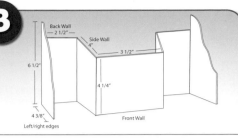

- Our castle measurements (small *Project Base & Backdrop*): Left / Right Edges (4 3/8"), Back Walls (2 1/2"), Side Walls (4"), Front Wall (3 1/2")
- Height: 6 1/2" (tallest point), 4 1/4" (shortest point).

4

- Design castle, then cut out with a hobby knife.
- Make new fold lines by indenting *Backdrop* with the blunt end of a paintbrush. (Fig. 3a)

5

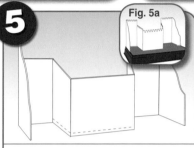

Fig. 5a

- Cut off 1/4" from bottom of *Backdrop* along side and front walls. This will allow the *Backdrop* to set flush on top of the *Project Base*.
- Test fit on *Project Base* and make needed adjustments. (Fig. 5a).

6

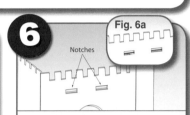

Fig. 6a

Notches

- Cut out crenellation and castle door.
- Cut out two notches on front wall.
- Cut a piece of round toothpick and glue into cutout. (Fig. 6a)
- Drawbridge chain will be attached to toothpicks in Step 19.

7

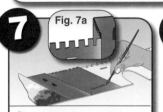

Fig. 7a

ℹ **Paint** (pg. 156-165)
- Paint front of castle cutout only. Include scenery, windows and details.
- Paint exposed foam edges black. (Fig. 7a)
- Let dry, then test fit on Project Base.

8

Fig. 8a

- Use excess *Backdrop* material for towers and tower tops. (Fig. 8a)
- Use a hobby knife to cut crenellation. Score fold lines with blunt end of a paintbrush.

9

ℹ **Contact Gluing Method** (pg. 169)
- Glue towers and tower tops in place using the Contact Gluing Method.
- Let dry.

10

Fig. 10a

- Cut two squares of cardstock for tower landing.
- Test fit, then cut a flap for ladders (Step 26). (Fig. 10a)
- Paint, let dry and glue in place.

11

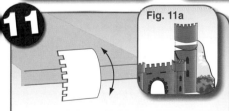

Fig. 11a

- To add side tower tops, cut out two pieces of *Backdrop* material for upper towers on back walls.
- Run along edge of a table to form curve.
- Cut two half circles to add support. (Fig. 11a)
- Paint to match castle. Let dry, then glue in place.

12

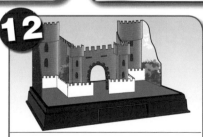

- Cut curtain wall out of *Backdrop* material.
- Test fit and make needed adjustments.

13

- Using a pencil, draw outline of moat on *ReadyGrass*.
- Remove castle and curtain wall.

14

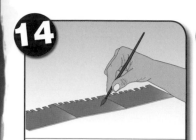

ℹ **Paint** (pg. 156-165)

• Paint front and back of curtain wall. Let dry.

TIP! Paint curtain wall to resemble the castle.

15

Fig. 15a

ℹ **Remove Turf** (pg. 114)

• Wet area inside moat outline. Scrape off turf with handle of *Foam Brush*.

• Paint moat with craft paint as desired. Let dry.

• Outline entire moat with *Project Glue*. Let dry. (Fig. 15a)

16

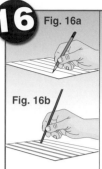

Fig. 16a

Fig. 16b

Fig. 16c

• Cut out a piece cardstock for drawbridge.

• Draw lines to represent wood planks on cardstock (Fig. 16a), then indent with dull end of paintbrush. (Fig. 16b)

• Cut five strips of cardstock for wooden cross sections.

• Align strips on backside of cardstock then glue in place. (Fig. 16c)

• Let dry, then paint as desired.

17

• Create a portcullis from flat toothpicks.

• Cut off point end and split in two for cross-sections.

• Glue together with *Project Glue*.

• Let dry, then paint as desired.

18

ℹ **Contact Gluing Method** (pg. 171)

• Test fit castle and curtain wall on *Project Base*. Make any final adjustments.

• Glue in place using the Contact Gluing Method.

• Let dry.

19

Fig. 19a

• Glue portcullis and drawbridge in place.

• Attach front end of drawbridge with craft wire.

• Glue top of wire to toothpicks glued in cutouts in front wall. (Fig. 19a)

TIP! Paint black lines on wire for a chain-like look.

20

allure   back

• Cut strips of *Backdrop* material to create the allure.

• Attach with *Project Glue*.

• Let dry.

21

back

ℹ **Paint** (pg. 156-165)

• Paint backside of castle as desired.

• Let dry.

22

ℹ **Project Glue in Spray Bottle** (pg. 170) **and Foliage Fiber** (pg. 118)

• Prepare *Foliage Fiber* per Basic Use instructions.

• Let dry.

• Glue to side of castle.

23

ℹ **Ground Cover** (pg. 116-125)

• Spray *Project Glue* where you want thicker areas of greenery. Sprinkle *Green Grass* over *Glue*. Spray again to seal.

• Attach *Bushes* and pebbles where desired with *Project Glue*.

24

ℹ **Realistic Water** (pg. 130)

• Pour *Realistic Water* slowly on moat area.

• Pull out to edges with *Stir Stick*.

• Let dry until clear (approx. 24 hrs.)

25

• On backside of castle, remove turf to make paths.

• Sprinkle additional *Accents* to add texture and spray with *Project Glue* to seal.

26

back

Ideas!

- Add required elements to your project from leftover materials and household items. See our diorama for ideas.
- Use excess *Backdrop* material (or foam board) to make a stable.
- Make a well from excess *Backdrop* material. Use toothpicks for posts and cardstock for well roof.
- Build a kitchen. Use cardstock for walls and excess *Backdrop* material for roof.

27

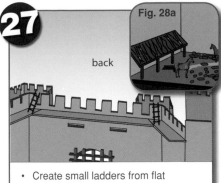

Fig. 28a

back

- Create small ladders from flat toothpicks.
- Attach miniature farm animals for a touch of realism. (Fig. 28a)

28

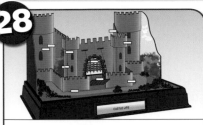

ℹ️ **Labels** (pg. 98-99)

- Label your project to point out the required elements.
- Print labels on cardstock and attach to craft wire or glue directly to element.
- Label front of Project Base.

Fun Fact!

The job of "taster" was one of the most dangerous. He tasted food before the royals to make sure it was not poisoned.

More Ideas!

Building a castle is easier than you think! Draw a "brick pattern" on Project Board, and then score the pattern with a hobby knife. This adds an authentic brick-look to the castle.

CASTLE LIFE

EGYPTIAN BURIAL ARTIFACTS

Here's what we used...

SCENEARAMA® Items

- **Sculpting Kit**
- **Plaster Cloth**
- **Small Project Base & Backdrop**

Household Items

- Balloon, 7"
- Corrugated Cardboard, 9" x 15"
- Cutting Surface
- Disposable Cup
- Foam Core Board
- Gold Craft Paint
- Hobby Knife
- Masking Tape
- Newspaper
- Pan for Water
- Pencil
- Sandpaper (medium grade)
- Scissors
- Styrofoam Ball, 1 1/2"
- Styrofoam Ball, 2 1/2"

Did you know?

Ancient Egyptians believed the body must be preserved (mummified) upon death to ensure rebirth. Preservation of the body included the removal of the stomach, intestines, liver and lungs, each were mummified and then placed in individual Canopic Jars. Items such as masks, amulets and furniture were placed with the body to provide divine protection and the same earthly luxuries in the afterlife.

Fun Fact!

Because the cobra was such a threatening creature in Egypt, the cobra symbol (uraeus) represented a powerful kingship.

Pharaoh's Mask

Canopic Jar

EGYPTIAN BURIAL ARTIFACTS

1
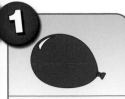
- Blow up balloon and tie a knot. (Have an adult help you with this step.)

NOTE: Do not blow balloon too full or mask will be too big for *Project Base*.

2

- Position cardboard behind balloon. Balloon should set below bottom edge of cardboard.
- Trace around balloon and draw a headdress outline.
- Cut out with hobby knife.
- Tape cardboard to balloon. (Fig. 2a)

3
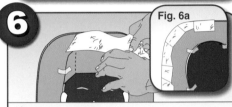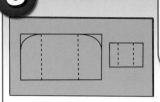
- Cut a chin beard and front section of headdress out of cardboard.
- Fold at dotted lines. (Fig. 3a)
- Test fit on balloon for proper size.

4
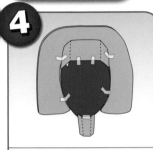
- Use masking tape to attach front portion of headdress and chin beard.

5
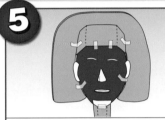
Sculpt (pg. 138-145)
- Using *Sculpting Clay*, sculpt nose, chin, ears, eyebrows and lips.
- Let dry.
- Once dry, use *Project Glue* to attach above pieces to balloon.
- Let dry.

6

Plaster Cloth (pg. 104-105)
- Cover front of mask with 2-3 layers of wet *Plaster Cloth* (3" strips), bumpy side up.
- Smooth each strip with wet fingers so *Cloth* conforms to shape and contours.
- Overlap edges of cardboard pad headdress by 1/2". (Fig. 6a)
- Do not cover back of balloon with *Plaster Cloth*.

7
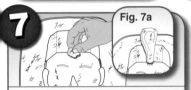
- Using wet *Plaster Cloth*, create a serpent for the headdress.
- Wad a piece of wet *Plaster Cloth* and place it on the headdress.
- Carefully press serpent onto wet *Plaster Cloth*. (Fig. 7a)
- Allow to set overnight or until hardened.

TIP! A fan will speed up drying time.

8
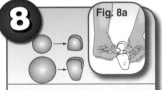
- Using a hobby knife and/or sandpaper, shape top of canopic jar from small Styrofoam ball and bottom from the larger ball.
- Attach together with *Project Glue*.
- Cover in wet *Plaster Cloth*. (Fig. 8a)
- Let dry.

9

- After *Plaster Cloth* is dry, carefully remove balloon and *Sculpting Clay*, then discard.

10
Paint (pg. 156-165)
- Before painting, draw desired design on mask with a pencil.
- Paint your mask and canopic jar as desired.
- Let dry.

11
Project Base & Backdrop (pg. 95-96)
- Design a *Backdrop* that best fits your mask.
- Cut out with a hobby knife.
- Paint front and back of *Backdrop,* as desired.

12

Easel Templates (pg. 174-175)
- Create an easel using foam core board for your mask.
- Cut out with a hobby knife.
- Paint easel, as desired.

NOTE: Mask can rest on *Backdrop* for extra support.

13

Contact Gluing Method (pg. 169)
- Attach easel to *Project Base* with the contact gluing method.
- Let dry.
- Make sure label area on *Project Base* is facing forward.

14

Labels (pg. 98-99)
- Glue *Backdrop* and canopic jar to *Project Base*
- Glue mask to easel.
- Label and add signage to your project.

MEDUSA

Here's what we used...

SCENE A RAMA® Items

- **Sculpting Kit**
- **Plaster Cloth**
- **Small Project Base & Backdrop**

Household Items

- Corrugated Cardboard, 7" x 10"
- Cutting Surface
- Disposable Cup
- Foam Core Board, 8" x 10"
- Hobby Knife
- Masking Tape
- Newspaper
- Pan for Water
- Pencil
- Pipe Cleaners
- Plastic Wrap
- Ruler
- Scissors

Did you know?

Greek mythology tells the story of Medusa, a beautiful woman who angered the goddess Athena. Athena turned Medusa into a monster, transforming her hair into a head of snakes. One glance at Medusa would turn a person to stone. Later, she was beheaded by Perseus, who gave her head to Athena to place on her shield.

Mythical

Fun Fact!
After Medusa was beheaded, Pegasus, a winged horse and her son by Poseidon, sprang from her blood.

MEDUSA

1

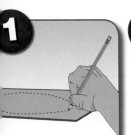

- Measure and cut a cardboard pad approx. 7" x 10".
- Draw outline of Medusa's head on cardboard pad.

2

- **📖 Newspaper Wads** (pg. 102-103)
- Place newspaper wads inside drawn outline and tape to hold.
- Tape newspaper wads together and to the cardboard pad.

NOTE: The height of the newspaper wads will determine depth of Mask.

3

- **📖 Sculpt** (pg. 138-145)
- Use *Sculpting Clay* to create nose, eyebrows and lips. Let dry.
- Glue or tape in place on mask.
- Cover mask loosely in plastic wrap and tape to cardboard.

4

- **📖 Plaster Cloth** (pg. 104-105)
- Fold 3" strip of wet *Plaster Cloth* in half (bumpy side out).
- Wrap around base of mask, folded edge next to cardboard pad.
- Smooth each strip with wet fingers to fill holes in *Cloth*.

5

- Cover rest of mask with wet *Plaster Cloth* (3" strips), bumpy side up.
- Smooth each strip with wet fingers to fill holes in *Cloth*.
- Tuck *Plaster Cloth* around eyebrows, lips, etc. to show contours.
- Apply 2 layers of *Plaster Cloth*.

6

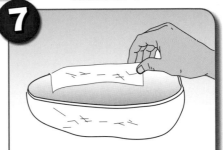

- Allow to set overnight or until hardened.
- Carefully remove mask from cardboard pad.
- Discard cardboard pad, plastic wrap, newspaper wads and *Sculpting Clay*.

7

- Add an additional layer of wet *Plaster Cloth* around edge of mask.
- Allow to set until hardened (approx. 30 minutes).

8

Fig. 8a

- Cut desired amount of pipe cleaners (snakes) in half.
- Starting 1" from top of pipe cleaner, wrap in wet *Plaster Cloth* strips and smooth with wet fingers.
- Bend pipe cleaner into snake-like shapes. (Fig. 8a)
- Pinch *Plaster Cloth* to form snake head. Add additional *Plaster Cloth*, if necessary.
- Attach snake to mask (see Step 9). Repeat for desired number of snakes.

9

Fig. 9a

- To attach snakes on mask, place snake on mask, then smooth a piece of wet *Plaster Cloth* over the end of pipe cleaner. Hold until setting begins.
- Use blunt end of of the sculpting tool to shape eyes. Pull a few threads from *Cloth* to make a tongue. (Fig. 9a)
- Prop up snakes to hold shape while drying.
- Allow to set overnight or until hardened.

10

- **📖 Paint** (pg. 156-165)
- Before painting, draw desired design on mask with a pencil.
- Paint your mask as desired.
- Let dry.

11

- **📖 Project Base & Backdrop** (pg. 95-96)
- Design a *Backdrop* that best fits your Mask.
- Cut out with a hobby knife.
- Paint *Backdrop* as desired.

12

- **📖 Easel Templates** (pg. 174-175)
- Create an easel for your Medusa mask.
- Cut out with a hobby knife.

13

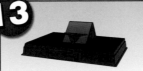

- **📖 Contact Gluing Method** (pg. 169)
- Attach easel to *Project Base* with the contact gluing method.
- Let dry.
- Make sure label area on *Project Base* faces forward.

14

- **📖 Labels** (pg. 98-99)
- Glue *Backdrop* to *Project Base*.
- Glue mask to easel.
- Label and add signage to your project.

NOTE: Rest mask on *Backdrop* for extra support.

BACTERIA CELL

Here's what we used...

SCENE A RAMA Items

- **Sculpting Kit**
- **Plaster Cloth**
- **Small Project Base & Backdrop**

Household Items

- Corrugated Cardboard, 5" x 10"
- Cutting Surface
- Disposable Cup
- Foam Core Board, 8" x 10"
- Masking Tape
- Newspaper
- Pan for Water
- Rolling Pin
- Scissors
- Wax Paper

Did you know?

Bacteria are a type of prokaryotic cell. Differing from eukaryotic cells, they lack a well-defined nuclei and membrane-bound organelles. They also have chromosomes made of a single closed DNA circle. Prokaryotic cells form three basic shapes: rod, spherical and spiral.

Fun Fact!

Bacteria have existed for 3.5 billion years, making them one of Earth's oldest living organisms.

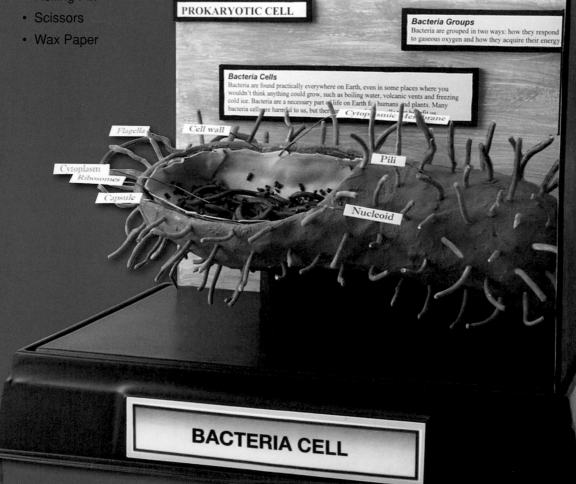

1

- Draw and color a cutaway view of a bacteria cell on the cardboard pad.
- Use this as your modeling reference.

2

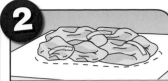

ℹ Newspaper Wads (pg. 102-103)
- Wad newspaper into bacteria cell shape (cell capsule).
- Tape wads together to hold shape.
- Discard cardboard.

NOTE: Cell should be approximately 9" long x 3" diameter.

3

ℹ Plaster Cloth (pg. 104-105)
- Cover entire newspaper wad shape with wet *Plaster Cloth* (3" strips), bumpy side up.
- Apply 2 layers of *Plaster Cloth*.
- Let dry until set (slightly damp).

4

Fig. 4a

- Using a hobby knife, cut opening in cell.
- Discard newspaper.
- Add layer of *Plaster Cloth* around edge. (Fig. 4a)

5

Fig. 5a

ℹ Sculpt (pg. 138-145)
- Flatten some *Sculpting Clay* between two sheets of wax paper.
- Cut a length of *Clay* to fit cell opening to form cell wall.
- Apply *Project Glue* and press in place around inside opening of cell. (Fig. 5a)

6

Fig. 6a

- Brush *Glue* on interior of cell and strip of *Clay*, then press remainder of flattened *Clay* into cavity.
- Align *Clay* with top of clay cell wall. (Fig. 6a)

7

- Roll *Clay* into tiny dots to form Ribosomes.
- Let dry.

8

Fig. 8a

- Roll a long section of *Clay* to form Nucleoid (circular DNA).
- Twist and overlap *Clay* to create DNA shape. (Fig. 8a)
- Let dry.

9

Fig. 9a

- Roll *Clay* into 1 1/2" pieces for Pili.
- Flatten one end for gluing. (Fig. 9a)
- Let dry.

10

- Roll *Clay* to form Flagellum.
- Cut one end flat for gluing.
- Let dry.

11

ℹ Paint (pg.156-165)
- Using craft paints, paint cell and cell parts as desired.
- Let dry.

12

Fig. 12a

- Glue some Ribosomes to Nucleoid.
- Glue remaining Ribosomes to interior of cell.
- Glue Nucleoid in place. (Fig. 12a)

13

Fig. 13a

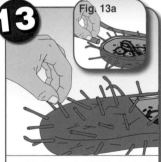

- Dip flat end of Pili in *Project Glue* and place on cell.
- Dip flat end of Flagellum in *Project Glue* and place on cell. (Fig. 13a)

14

ℹ Project Base & Backdrop (pg. 95-96)
- Design a *Backdrop* that best fits your cell.
- Cut out with a hobby knife.
- Paint front and back of *Backdrop* as desired.

15

ℹ Easel Templates (pg. 174-175)
- Design an easel using foam core board.
- Cut out with a hobby knife.

16

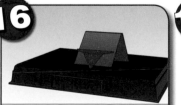

ℹ Contact Gluing Method (pg. 169)
- Using the Contact Gluing Method, attach easel to *Project Base*.
- Let dry.
- Make sure label area on *Project Base* faces forward.

17

ℹ Labels (pg. 98-99)
- Glue *Backdrop* to *Project Base*.
- Glue cell to easel.
- Label and add signage to your project.

BRAIN CELL

Here's what we used...

SCENE A RAMA® Items

- **Sculpting Kit**
- **Plaster Cloth**
- **Small Project Base & Backdrop**

Household Items

- Corrugated Cardboard, 10" x 10"
- Cutting Surface
- Disposable Cup
- Foam Core Board, 8" x 10"
- Masking Tape
- Pan for Water
- Plastic Wrap
- Rolling Pin
- Scissors
- Wax Paper

Did you know?

One of the most common cells in the brain are neurons. Neurons are the cells that store and process information. Information is transmitted through electrochemical signals between the brain and nervous system. Neurons communicate with each other through a process called synapsis. There are approximately 100 billion neurons in the brain.

Fun Fact!

The average number of neurons in an octopus brain is about 300 million.

1

- Sketch a Neuron on a piece of cardboard.
- Cover cardboard with plastic wrap and tape to hold.

TIP! Research cells, then print a picture to use as a reference.

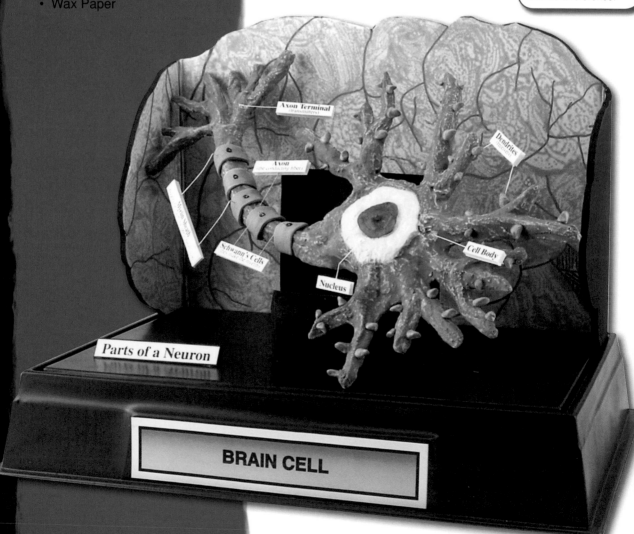

Parts of a Neuron

Axon Terminal (transmitters)

Dendrites

Axon (the conducting fibers)

Myelin Sheath

Schwann's Cells

Nucleus

Cell Body

BRAIN CELL

2

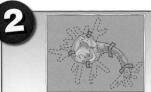

ℹ **Newspaper Wads** (pg. 102-103)
- Using your drawing as a guide, wad a half sheet of newspaper to create center cell body (Soma) shape.
- Wad another half sheet of newspaper to create the elongated (Axon) shape.
- Use masking tape to attach the two pieces together.

3

ℹ **Plaster Cloth** (pg. 104-105)
- Cover the entire cell shape with wet *Plaster Cloth* (3" strips), bumpy side up.
- Apply 2 layers of *Cloth*.

4

Fig. 4a

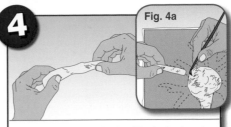

- Form Axon Terminals with pinched and formed strips of wet *Plaster Cloth*.
- Brush water on area of cell body before placing each wet strip of *Plaster Cloth*. (Fig. 4a)
- Pinch and mold wet *Plaster Cloth* for desired shape. Hold strip in place on cell until setting begins.

5

- Continue placing strips as in Step 4 until satisfied with look of cell.
- Let dry.

6

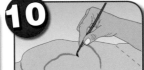

ℹ **Sculpt** (pg. 138-145)
- Pinch off small pieces of *Sculpting Clay* and form into Dendrite shapes.
- Use *Project Glue* to attach to Axon Terminals around cell body.

7

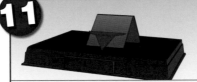

- Flatten a small amount *Clay* with rolling pin (approx. 1/16" thick) on a sheet of wax paper. Cut *Clay* into rectangular slices to create Myelin Sheath.
- Wrap around Axon and pinch together.
- Add a drop of *Project Glue*, if desired.

NOTE: Be sure to leave space between clay Myelin Sheaths to account for Nodes of Ranvier.

8

- Flatten clay in a circle to create Nucleus.
- Cut a small circle.
- Attach to cell body with *Project Glue*.
- Let dry.

9

ℹ **Paint** (pg. 156-165)
- Using *Project Paints*, paint cell as desired.

10

ℹ **Project Base & Backdrop** (pg. 95-96)
- Design a *Backdrop* that best fits your cell.
- Cut out with a hobby knife.
- Paint *Backdrop* as desired.

11

ℹ **Easel Templates** (pg. 174-175) and **Contact Gluing Method** (pg. 169)
- Design an easel using foam core board.
- Cut out with a hobby knife.
- Using the Contact Gluing Method, attach easel to *Project Base*.
- Let dry.
- Make sure label area on *Project Base* faces forward.

12

ℹ **Labels** (pg. 98-99)
- Glue *Backdrop* to *Project Base*.
- Glue cell to easel.
- Label and add signage to your project.

More Ideas!

Use newspaper wads to form the basic shape, then cover in Plaster Cloth to create this Splitting Cell project. The organelles and parent cell were made using Sculpting Clay and Project Paints from the Sculpting Kit.

GEYSERS

Here's what we used...

SCENE A RAMA® Items

- **Water Diorama Kit**
- **Casting Plaster**
- **Large Project Base & Backdrop**

Household Items

- Corrugated Cardboard, 16 1/4" x 11" (2)
- Cotton Balls (or Polyester Fiberfill)
- Craft Paints and Brushes
- Cutting Surface
- Disposable Cup
- Drinking Straw
- Foil
- Hobby Knife
- Masking Tape
- Measuring Spoons
- Mixing Bowl
- Pencil

Did you know?

A geyser begins with molten rock superheating groundwater. Steam and boiling water rise through rock layers and collect in a chamber. The heated water cannot expand because of the hard rock, so when the chamber is full, the water has no where to go but up. Geysers first emit a jet of steam, followed by water.

GEYSERS

1

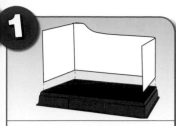

- Draw terrain profile on *Backdrop* material and cut out with a hobby knife.
- Test fit in grooves on *Project Base*, then attach with *Project Glue*.

2

Fig. 2a

- Using a piece of cardboard, measure and cut a shelf for geyser display area inside *Backdrop*.
- Draw location of geysers, hot springs, mudpots, limestone rock formation, etc. (Fig. 2a)

3

- Test fit shelf with *Backdrop*. Position shelf so it is level with lowest section of *Backdrop*.
- Mark underneath shelf on *Backdrop* to note location for shelf supports (Step 5).

4

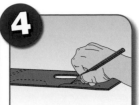

- Trim cardboard if necessary for best fit.
- Cut out hot springs with a hobby knife.
- We made two hot springs.

5

Fig. 5a

- Create Shelf Supports by cutting strips of *Side Panel* and gluing at marked location level around inside perimeter of *Backdrop*.
- Rest shelf on shelf supports. Use *Project Glue* to attach. (Fig. 5a)

6

- Create Support Pillars by cutting strips of *Side Panel* to support underneath shelf.
- Attach with masking tape.

7

- Cut a piece of cardboard to fit front of diorama and glue in place.
- Mark and cut out area for front hot spring.

8

ℹ **Newspaper Wads** (pg. 102-103)
- Arrange newspaper wads into desired mountain range shape.
- Tape to hold in place. Do not place tape on front panel or *Backdrop* material.

9

ℹ **Plaster Cloth** (pg. 104-105) and **Edging** (pg. 106)
- Cover newspaper wads and top of diorama with wet *Plaster Cloth* (3" strips), bumpy side up.
- Smooth plaster with wet fingers to fill holes in *Cloth*.

TIP! Cover front panel with paper towels to help keep it clean.

10

- Cut a piece of *Plaster Cloth* larger (on all sides) than hole cut for hot springs.
- Dip *Cloth* in water and place over hole, bumpy side up.
- Using a pencil, push down *Plaster Cloth* slowly. Leave about 1/2" of *Cloth* around edges.
- Smooth *Cloth* for desired shape. Add additional layer of *Plaster Cloth*, if desired.
- Form second spring in same manner.

11

ℹ **Casting Plaster** (pg. 108)
- Mix a small batch of *Casting Plaster* per Basic Use instructions.
- Pour *Casting Plaster* onto foil. Flatten top with the *Stir Stick*.
- Let dry.

12

Fig. 12a

- When *Casting Plaster* is dry, break into desired shapes for limestone rock formations.
- Stack pieces and attach together with *Project Glue*. (Fig. 12a)

13

- Prepare another batch of *Casting Plaster*.
- Dab *Casting Plaster* over *Plaster Cloth*.
- Create high and low areas for desired terrain effect.
- Form waterways with edge of *Stir Stick*.

14

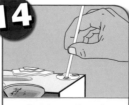

- Create mudpots by dabbing on a thick circle of prepared *Casting Plaster*.
- Place a straw in *Casting Plaster* and blow gently. This will create the bubbling effect.

15

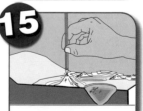

- Create geyser mounds with small wads of wet *Plaster Cloth*.
- Create hole in geysers with the tip of a pencil.

16
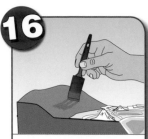

ⓘ Earth Undercoat
(pg. 171)
- Brush diluted *Earth Undercoat* on mountain area.
- Save some *Earth Undercoat* for step 18.

17

- Paint terrain, geysers, hot springs, mudpots, etc. with craft paints.
- Be creative! Use pictures of actual hot springs for color inspiration.

18

ⓘ Talus (pg. 123-125)
- Pour crushed *Talus* into remaining *Earth Undercoat*.
- Mix with *Stir Stick*.
- Remove *Talus*, and let dry on newspaper.
- When dry, attach along base of mountain.

19

ⓘ Project Glue in Spray Bottle (pg. 170)
- Spray diluted *Project Glue* on desired greenery areas.
- Sprinkle *Green Grass* heavily on wet glue.

20

ⓘ Ground Cover
(pg. 116-125)
- Sprinkle darker *Accents* lightly over *Green Grass* to model realistic coloring.
- Glue *Shrubs* in desired areas.

21

ⓘ Conifer Trees (pg. 127)
- Use *Foliage Fiber* to make conifer trees.
- Attach with *Project Glue*.

22

ⓘ Realistic Water
(pg. 130)
- Pour *Realistic Water* slowly on water areas.
- Brush on hot springs, rock formations, mudpots and other areas to give a wet look.
- Let dry until clear (approx. 24 hours).

23

- Pull and stretch cotton balls (or polyester fiber fill) into smoke shapes.
- Spray heavily with diluted *Project Glue*.
- When dry, glue to geysers with *Project Glue*.

24

- Paint front of diorama to resemble earth layers and ground water.
- Use a pencil to mark cracks and crevices.

TIP! Glue stretched cotton balls to represent steam collecting in rock chambers.

25

ⓘ Labels (pg. 98-99)
- Paint outside of *Backdrop* and touch up any problem areas.
- Label and add signage to your project.

More Ideas!

This Geyser project was done by our testing student Greg. "I love how my project turn out, and I had the best time!"

LUNGS AND SMOKING

Here's what we used...

SCENE·A·RAMA® Items

- **Ripplin'Water Kit**
- **Plaster Cloth**
- **Project Glue**
- **Large Project Base & Backdrop**

Household Items

- Corrugated Cardboard, 12" x 12"
- Craft Paints and Brushes
- Cutting Surface
- Dispoable Cup
- Foam Core Board, 8" x 10" (2)
- Hobby Knife
- Newspaper
- Pan for Water

Did you know?

In the United States, lung cancer is the cause of more cancer related deaths than colon, prostate, ovarian, lymph and breast cancers combined. Cigarette smokers are at the greatest risk of developing lung cancer, and the risk increases with the length of time and amount of cigarettes smoked.

Fun Fact!
Our lungs consist of approximately 90% air and only 10% tissue.

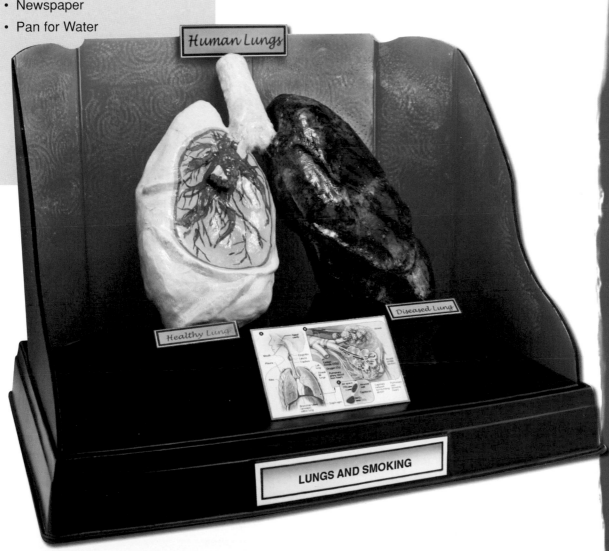

Human Lungs

Healthy Lung

Diseased Lung

LUNGS AND SMOKING

1

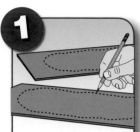

ℹ️ **Lungs Template** (pg. 188)
- Trace lung templates on cardboard, then cut out.

2

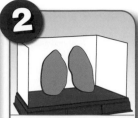

- Test fit lung cutouts on *Project Base* with *Backdrop* in grooves.
- Easels will add height to lungs.
- Enlarge or reduce lung size if desired.

3

ℹ️ **Newspaper Wads** (pg. 102)
- Fill in outlines with newspaper wads.
- Form wads into lung shapes.
- Tape to hold.

4

- Starting at the outer edges, roll a sheet of newspaper toward the center.
- Cut the rolled newspaper half way up the sheet where the two sides meet in the middle.

5

- Form rolled newspaper into inverted "Y" shape.
- Tape to hold, then cut to fit lungs.

6

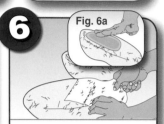

Fig. 6a

ℹ️ **Plaster Cloth** (pg. 104-105)
- Cover newspaper wads and back of cardboard with wet *Plaster Cloth*.
- Smooth an indent on top of right lung for cutaway area. (Fig. 6a)

7

- Use small strips of wet *Plaster Cloth* to define lobes.
- Place on lungs while *Plaster Cloth* is still wet.
- Outline cutaway area with strips of wet *Plaster Cloth*.

8

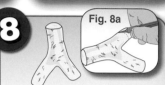

Fig. 8a

- Cover newspaper "Y" in 2 layers of wet *Plaster Cloth*. Overlap edges for a finished look.
- Test fit lungs while *Plaster Cloth* is wet. Trim for a proper fit. (Fig.8a)
- Let dry.

9

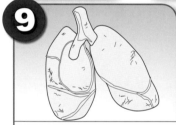

- Attach "Y" to lungs one side at a time.
- Attach with *Project Glue* or strips of wet *Plaster Cloth*.
- Hold in place until setting begins.
- Let dry.

10

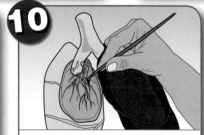

- Paint lungs as desired with craft paints.
- We painted a healthy lung and a diseased lung.
- Let dry.

11

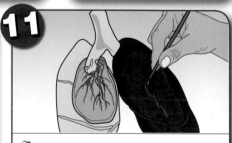

ℹ️ **Shiny Areas** (pg. 132)
- Brush *Realistic Water* over painted lungs.
- This will give the lungs a shiny, wet appearance.
- Let dry 24 hours.

12

ℹ️ **Water Effects** (pg. 132)
- Using the *Stir Stick*, dab *Water Effects* along blood vessels.
- This will give them a raised appearance.
- Let dry until clear.

NOTE! Make sure *Realistic Water* is dry before applying *Water Effects*.

13

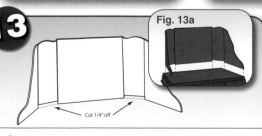

Fig. 13a

Cut 1/4" off

ℹ️ **Project Base & Backdrop** (pg. 95-96)
- Design a *Backdrop* that best fits your diorama.
- Attach *Backdrop* to *Project Base* using *Project Glue*. (Fig. 13a)

TIP! Create a unique design by cutting 1/4" off bottom of backdrop as illustrated. Score new fold lines with blunt end of a paintbrush.

14

ℹ️ **Easel Template** (pg. 174)
- Create two easels using foam board and the Easel Template.
- If desired, paint foam board to match your project.

15

ℹ **Contact Gluing Method**
(pg. 169)

- Use *Project Glue* and
  Contact Gluing Method to
  attach easels to *Project
  Base*.
- Attach lungs to easels.
- Let dry.

16

ℹ **Labels** (pg. 98-99)

- Label and add signage to your
  project.

Helpful Hint
Paint Realistic Water
over an anatomy
project to give it a wet
appearance.

More Ideas!

Visit the Tips, Techniques & Templates
section for loads of ideas on how to add
impressive details to a science project or
anatomy diorama.

Science Projects

CROSS-SECTION VOLCANO

Here's what we used...

SCENE·A·RAMA® Items

- **Mountain Diorama Kit**
- **Small Project Base & Backdrop**

Household Items

- Cardstock, 3" x 5"
- Cotton Ball
- Craft Paints & Brushes
- Cutting Surface
- Disposable Cup
- Hobby Knife
- Masking Tape
- Measuring Spoons
- Newspaper
- Pan for Water
- Scissors

Did you know?

A volcano erupts when magma (molten rock) rises into the Earth's crust and collects in a space or pocket called a magma chamber. As the magma boils, pressure builds until the magma is pushed toward the surface. Magma breaks the surface via vent pipes.

Fun Fact!

The world's most active volcano, Kilauea (pronounced kill-O-ey-ah), is located on the big island of Hawaii. It has erupted almost continuously since 1983.

CROSS-SECTION VOLCANO

1
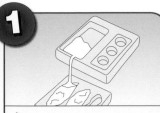
- **Rock Castings** (pg. 108-110)
- Mix and use *Casting Plaster* per Basic Use instructions.
- Pour into *Rock Mold*, let set for 30-40 minutes.

2

Fig. 2a
- Using a hobby knife, cut one side off the *Backdrop*. (Fig. 2a)
- Make a cardboard pad by cutting a cardboard *Side Panel* 10 3/8" x 7 1/8". (Fig. 2a)

3

Fig. 3a
- Cut *Backdrop* material into panel for cross-section area.
- Score down the center of panel.
- Attach to cardboard pad with masking tape. (Fig. 3a)

4

- **Newspaper Wads** (pg. 102)
- Arrange newspaper wads behind panel on cardboard pad into desired terrain shape.
- Tape newspaper wads to hold in place.
- Newspaper wads must not protrude over cardboard pad.

5
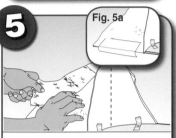
Fig. 5a
- **Plaster Cloth** (pg. 104-105) and **Edging** (pg. 106)
- Cover newspaper wads and cardboard pad with wet *Plaster Cloth* (3" strips), bumpy side up.
- Overlap edges of cardboard pad by 1/2". (Fig. 5a)

6

- While *Plaster Cloth* is damp, test fit on *Project Base* with *Backdrop* in grooves.
- If it interferes with *Backdrop*, make adjustments.
- Remove from *Project Base*.

7

- **Attach and Blend Rocks** (pg. 109-110)
- Attach rock castings in desired locations while *Plaster Cloth* is still damp.
- Let dry.
NOTE: Do not drip glue or plaster on rock face.

8

- Hold *Volcano Tube* in place.
- Set small, wet wads of *Plaster Cloth* around base of *Volcano Tube*.
- Stack wads until approx. 3/8" high.
- Let dry, then remove *Tube*.

9

- **Leopard Spot** (pg. 160)
- Dilute *Rock Colors*.
- Paint rock castings with the Leopard Spot paint technique.

10
- **Dilute Earth Undercoat** (pg. 171)
- Brush diluted *Earth Undercoat* over entire terrain (avoid rocks).
- Let dry.
NOTE: Save some diluted *Earth Undercoat* for Step 12.

11

- Paint rock layers, magma chamber, vents, fissures and/or other required information on the cutaway panel.
- Paint *Plaster Cloth* area in front of cutaway panel. Let dry.

12
- **Talus** (pg. 123-124)
- Pour *Talus* into remaining *Earth Undercoat*.
- Mix with *Stir Stick*.
- Let dry on newspaper.

13

- **Foliage Fiber** (pg. 118)
- Prepare *Foliage Fiber* per Basic Use instructions.

14

Fig. 14a
- **Ground Cover** (pg. 116-125)
- Spray diluted *Project Glue* on backside of volcano where you want greenery.
- Sprinkle with *Green Grass* and other *Accents*.
- Use *Project Glue* to attach prepared *Foliage Fiber* where desired. (Fig. 14a)

15

- Use *Project Glue* to attach *Shrubs* and *Talus* where desired.
- Spray ground cover with *Project Glue* to seal.

89

16

- Pull a cotton ball until very thin and lacy.
- Spray with diluted *Project Glue*. Let dry.
- Dab on black paint. Let dry, then glue in place.

17

ℹ️ **Project Base & Backdrop** (pg. 95-97)
- Glue cross-section volcano to *Project Base*.
- Paint as desired.
- Attach *Backdrop* with *Project Glue*.
- Design a *Backdrop* that best fits your diorama.
- Make sure label area faces forward.

18

ℹ️ **Labels** (pg. 98-99)
- Use cardstock and extra *Backdrop* material to make informational labels.
- Add signage to front of diorama.
- Replace *Volcano Tube*.
- See page 171 for Eruption Mixture.

More Volcanoes!

Get creative! Design your own unique Volcano project.

GEOLOGY

ERUPTING VOLCANO

CINDER CONES

COASTAL ERUPTION

A⁺ ideas!

ENERGY EFFICIENCY

Here's what we used...

SCENE A RAMA® Items

- **Mountain Diorama Kit**
- **Scene Setters: Alternative Energy**
- **Small Project Base & Backdrop**

Household Items

- Black Construction Paper
- Cutting Surface
- Disposable Cups
- Hobby Knife
- Masking Tape
- Measuring Spoons
- Sandpaper - Medium Grade
- Newspaper
- Pan for Water
- Scissors

Did you know?

Wind turbines convert the kinetic energy of wind into mechanical energy, creating a renewable energy source. Modern wind turbines are often found on wind farms to commercially produce electric power.

Fun Fact!

An increasing number of homes across the United States are becoming environmentally friendly by using renewable energy sources, like wind.

Helpful Hint

Use our diorama as a guide to create your own unique energy efficient home.

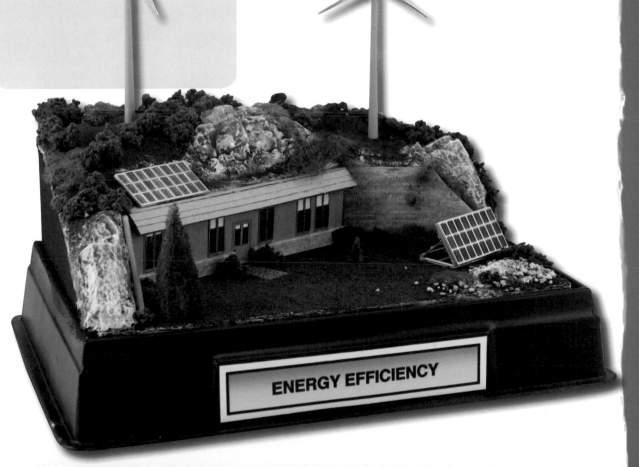

ENERGY EFFICIENCY

1

ℹ Rock Castings (pg. 108)
- Mix and use *Casting Plaster* per Basic Use instructions.
- Pour into *Rock Mold*, let set for 30-40 minutes.

TIP! For a variety of rock sizes, fill mold less than half full and prop at an angle until set.

2

ℹ Project Base & Backdrop (pg. 95-97)
- Design outline of terrain from *Backdrop*.
- Cut out with hobby knife.
- Test fit on *Project Base*, then attach with *Project Glue*.
- Make sure label area faces forward.

3

- Using a section of *Side Panel*, create desired cutaway mountain area.
- Include a space for house facade and retaining walls.
- Cut out with a hobby knife.
- Attach with masking tape.

4

ℹ Newspaper Wads (pg. 102)
- Arrange newspaper wads into desired terrain shape behind cardboard.
- Tape to hold shape.

5

ℹ Plaster Cloth (pg. 104-105)
- Using sandpaper, rough up flat area of *Base*.
- Cover diorama with wet *Plaster Cloth* (3" strips), bumpy side up (do not cover grooves in base).
- Smooth each strip with wet fingers. Let dry until slightly damp.

6

ℹ Attach and Blend Rocks (pg. 109-110)
- Attach rocks to terrain.
- Poke 1" strips of wet *Plaster Cloth* around rock edges to fill in gaps.
- Let dry.

7

ℹ Leopard Spot (pg. 160)
- Dilute *Rock Colors*.
- Paint rocks with Leopard Spot technique.

NOTE: Save some diluted *Rock Colors* for Steps 9 and 14.

8

ℹ Earth Undercoat (pg. 171)
- Brush diluted *Earth Undercoat* over entire terrain (avoid rocks).
- Let dry.

9

ℹ Color Talus (pg. 124)
- Pour *Talus* into remaining *Rock Colors*.
- Mix with *Stir Stick*.
- Remove *Talus*, and let dry on newspaper.

10

ℹ Project Glue in Spray Bottle (pg. 170)
- Spray diluted *Project Glue* on desired greenery areas.
- Sprinkle *Green Grass* on *Glue*.
- Sprinkle *Accents*, individually or as a mixture over *Green Grass*.
- Spray with *Project Glue* to seal.

11

ℹ Conifer Trees (pg. 127)
- Make Conifer Trees from *Foliage Fiber*.
- Attach *Talus* with *Project Glue*.
- Attach *Shrubs* with *Project Glue*.

12

ℹ Buildings & Structures (pg. 147-155)
- Use a section of *Side Panel* to create house facade.
- Cut out with a hobby knife.
- Paint, if desired.
- Use a fine-tip marker to outline window and doors.

13

Back

- Cut out windows with hobby knife.
- Glue small strips of white paper to backside of house facade as window coverings.
- Cut out black construction paper and cover windows.
- Glue house facade in place.

14

- Using a section of *Backdrop*, cut out retaining walls and any facade embellishments (roof, trim, etc.).
- Stain with diluted *Rock Colors*.
- Attach with *Project Glue*.
- Add additional landscape details.

TIP! See Brick Pattern in Buildings & Structures (pg. 152) to add a brick design if desired.

15

ℹ Labels (pg. 98-99)
- Use *Project Glue* to attach *Scene Setters* in desired areas.
- Poke a hole in terrain to install *Wind Turbines* or use optional base.
- Label and add signage to your project.

Tips, Techniques &TEMPLATES

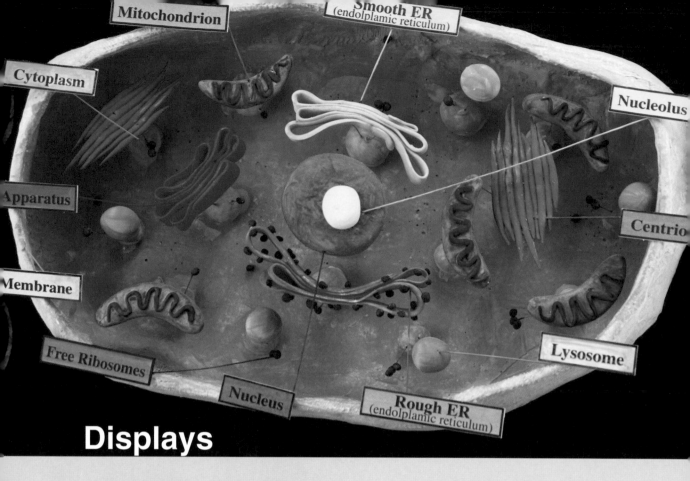

Mitochondrion

Smooth ER
(endolplamic reticulum)

Cytoplasm

Nucleolus

Apparatus

Centrio

Membrane

Free Ribosomes

Nucleus

Rough ER
(endolplamic reticulum)

Lysosome

Displays

ShowBox

The ShowBox is perfect for shoebox projects, three-dimensional displays and dioramas. It is sturdy enough to display your project on a shelf for years to come!

Project Area: 13" L x 8-1/2"H x 4-1/2"D

Basic Use

1. Decorate inside the ShowBox, adding imaginative details to enhance your project. Add color with Project Paint, spray paint, markers, crayons, ready-made backgrounds and more.

2. Paint outside the ShowBox for a clean, finished look.

   • Use the included labels to display information about your project.

   • Get creative! Display outside the ShowBox.

- ShowBox Ideas

Display projects horizontally...   vertically...   or as a view from above.

Project Base & Backdrop

The Project Base and Backdrop sets the foundation for an amazing, professional-looking project.

Small Base Project Area: 7 3/8" W x 10 3/4" L
Large Base Project Area: 10 3/4" W x 16 1/4" L

Basic Use

1. **Project Base**

   - Cover the Project Base with a ReadyGrass Sheet and landscape materials.
   - Add a terrain profile to the Project Base using newspaper wads and Plaster Cloth.
   - Use the Project Base to display visual aids.

TIPS!

For extra heavy projects, reinforce the Project Base by gluing a piece of corrugated cardboard to the underside.

Cover edges of Project Base with newspaper or paper towels to keep it clean while working on your project.

The molded area on the front is designed to display an informational label.

2. **Backdrop**

- Design a Backdrop that shows-off your project and creativity.

- Cut the Backdrop with a hobby knife.

- The Backdrop is a great place to list important information about your project. (See Labels pg. 98-99)

- When using the Backdrop, do NOT cover the grooves in the Project Base with project materials. The Backdrop must be able to fit in the grooves.

- Paint the backside of the Backdrop for a clean, finished look. (See Paint pg. 156-165)

- Go to scenearama.com for printable backgrounds (See Ideas & Tips).

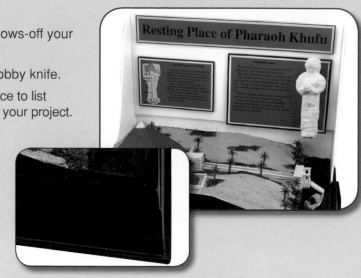

- How to Decorate Your Backdrop

Incorporate the Backdrop into your project.

Using a hobby knife, cut the Backdrop into an interesting shape or design.

Paint the Backdrop with Project Paints (or craft paint).

Decorate the Backdrop with color markers or glitter.

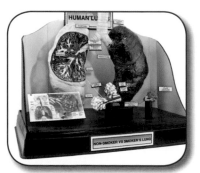

Use spray paint to paint front and back of Backdrop Use Project Paint to paint edges.

Attach a pre-printed background or photos. Make frames and labels from excess Backdrop material.

- Stencil

Make a stencil for a uniform design.

- Practice different patterns on scratch paper. Draw favorite pattern on cardstock and cut out.

- Trace your stencil on one Backdrop side panel.

- Flip the stencil over and trace it on the opposite side. Using a hobby knife, cut out design.

- Add Dimension to Your Backdrop

Add a snow scene. (See Add Snow to Backdrop pg. 135)

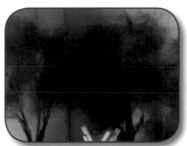

Glue Foliage to hand-painted tree trunks. (See Tree Foliage pg. 118)

Attach three-dimensional objects to the Backdrop. (See Plaster Cloth pg. 104-105)

- More Backdrop Ideas

Incorporate the Backdrop into your landscape.

Show before and after scenarios.

Add a top to give the illusion of an enclosed space.

Easels

An easel is a great way to present a project. Display an anatomy project, a decorative mask and much more!

Basic Use

Design an easel that supports the size of your project.

Rest projects against the Backdrop for extra support.

See the Template section (pg. 174-175) for simple easel patterns.

Labels

Creative labels turn a ho-hum project into something spectacular!

Basic Use

1. Label the Project Base

- When using supplied Project Labels, display information on the shiny side.

- Use markers, computer printer or label maker to create clever labels.

2. Label Project Items

- Design a label on Construction Board (cardstock). Use a computer printer, markers, colored pencils, etc.

- Use scissors to cut out label. Attach with Project Glue.

- Project Board Labels

Use Project Board (foam core board) to create professional-looking labels.

Design your label and add text. Add a colorful border. Print labels on copy paper.

Use Project Glue to attach the label to a piece of Project Board.

Cut out using a hobby knife. Use fine grade sandpaper to sand edges smooth.

If desired, paint edges of Project Board black or a color to match the label.

Glue Project Board label to Backdrop or parts of project in preferred location.

Allow to dry.

- Paint Wire to Match Labels

Use Project Glue to attach label to Project Wire.

Paint Project Wire same color as label.

Glue other end of Project Wire to the corresponding object.

1. A variety of foliage materials model a realistic forest. (See Trees page 126-129)

2. Crush and color Talus to match the region you are modeling. (See Talus page 123)

3. Brush Realistic Water on rock castings to model water seeping through a rock cliff.

4. Color rock castings with Rock Colors pigment, using the Leopard Spot paint technique. (See Leopard Spot page 160)

5. Create a silt river bottom by pouring Casting Plaster along the water area. (See Casting Plaster page 108)

6. Use natural materials like twigs and sticks as river debris or deadfall.

7. Create a flowing river by adding Plaster Cloth to the river bottom. (See Flowing River pg. 106)

Terrain

Newspaper Wads

Newspaper wads are the foundation for projects using Plaster Cloth. Use them to form all sorts of terrain shapes, such as mountains, valleys, meadows or rolling hills. You can also use newspaper wads to form a mask, cell, freeform sculptures and much more.

Basic Use

1. Start with a full-sized sheet of newspaper. Wad by rolling edges under while turning newspaper sheet in a clockwise motion. Create a pillow or large potato shape.

2. Stack wads in desired terrain formation. Hold formation in place with masking tape. The number of newspaper wads you need to make will depend on the size and shape of your project.

NOTE: Use small newspaper wads or damp paper towels to fill in gaps.

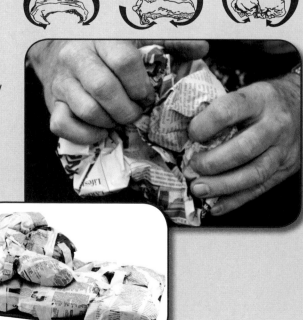

– More Newspaper Wad Projects

Here are more project ideas using newspaper wads and Plaster Cloth.

1. Masks

- Arrange newspaper wads into mask shape.
- Attach small pieces of newspaper for eyebrows, lips, nose, etc.

2. Cell Structures

- Make a hollow shell or a cutaway project, such as a cell, igloo or mask. Be sure to cover the newspaper wads with plastic wrap before applying Plaster Cloth. This will keep newsprint from sticking to the Plaster Cloth.

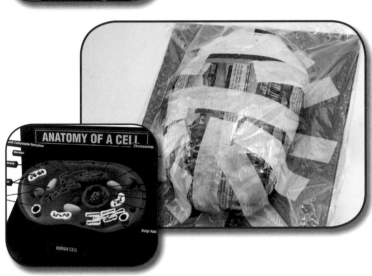

3. Abstract Shapes

- For very smooth surfaces, tape a folded sheet of newspaper flat on newspaper wads or to a cardboard structure.

Plaster Cloth

Sculpting with Plaster Cloth is the easiest way to create a lightweight, hard surface. Lay wet Plaster Cloth on newspaper wads to create terrain surface. You can also form over other objects, such as foil, a balloon, wire mesh and Styrofoam. It sets quickly and can be painted when dry.

NOTE: Be sure to cover your project area with newspaper or appropriate table covering. Plaster Cloth can be messy!

Basic Use

1. Cut Plaster Cloth into 3" strips. Fill a shallow pan with approximately 1" of cold water. Run a strip quickly through water and apply to project. Do NOT soak in water or cloth will lose a lot of plaster.

2. Start along one side and lay Plaster Cloth bumpy side up. Spread the plaster with wet fingers. Smooth out all the Plaster bumps until holes in Cloth are filled. Work efficiently, as the plaster sets quickly.

1. Repeat process, overlapping each strip by 50%. This forms a seamless, double-layer of Plaster Cloth.

2. Overlap edge of cardboard pad 1/2". Let Plaster Cloth dry four to six hours. Drying times depend on heat and humidity.

TIPS!

- A fan will accelerate drying time.
- Depending on the project, you may need some smaller strips of Plaster Cloth.
- Create an extra hard shell: add multiple layers of Plaster Cloth.
- For hard-to-reach areas, place dry Plaster Cloth on desired area, then spray with water. Smooth out plaster with wet fingers.
- When creating a water area, any holes in the Plaster Cloth not filled in with plaster will let Realistic Water leak through to the base. Smooth and spread wet plaster bumps with wet fingers.
- When having trouble smoothing plaster, add an additional layer of Cloth.
- When finished, pour water from pan and empty excess plaster into trash, not down the drain.

- Terrain Profile

Create a terrain profile from Backdrop material. Fill the terrain profile with newspaper wads.

Design a terrain profile using the Backdrop material. The front panel is cut from the top center section. The edges on the front panel must align with the side flaps on Backdrop.

Test fit on Project Base, and make necessary adjustments. Glue Backdrop material in grooves on Project Base.

Arrange newspaper wads into terrain shape. Cover with wet Plaster Cloth. (See Plaster Cloth pg. 104)

Continued on pg. 106

Continued from pg. 105

NOTE:

- If you want to use the Backdrop as a backdrop, cardboard Side Panels can be used to create the terrain profile instead.
- Attach Side Panels around inside edge of grooves on

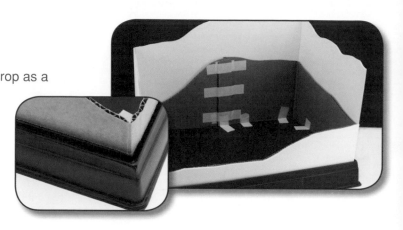

- Edging

Use this technique to create a clean edge on terrain projects or cutaway projects.

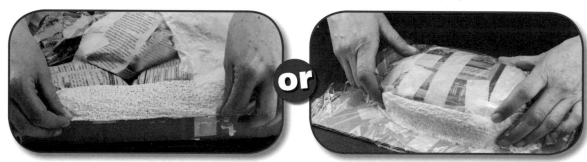

Fold Plaster Cloth strip in half lengthwise, bumpy side out. Dip in water and lay folded edge flush along terrain edge.

Or, wrap around the base of a project. Smooth and spread Plaster with wet fingers to flatten and fill in holes.

- Flowing River

These effects look great with Realistic Water!

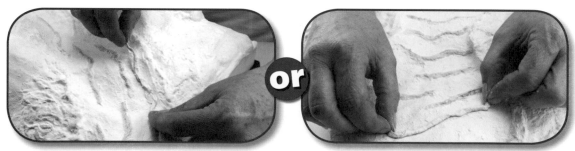

Brush or spray water on river bed area. Roll thin strips of wet Plaster Cloth. Lay strips lengthwise along river to model the current.

Lay strips across river to model ripples or changes in elevation. Blend strips into river-bed by pinching and smoothing the wet cloth.

TIPS!

- See Paint (pg. 161) for tips on painting water areas.
- Create white caps by leaving top of Plaster Cloth strips white.

- More Plaster Cloth Ideas

- **Terrain Details**

  Use small pieces of Plaster Cloth to create terrain details, like erosion, boulders or defining edges of a water fall. (See Environmental Effects diorama on pg. 23.)

- **Add Details to Masks**

  Create a head full of snakes! Wrap wet Plaster Cloth around pipe cleaners. (See Medusa mask on pg. 76.)

- **Accentuate Details**

  On this diorama, we accentuated the lobes of the lungs. (See Lungs and Smoking diorama pg. 85)

- **Use A Ballon**

  A balloon is a great tool when a project has to be perfectly round, as with a mask or an igloo. (See Igloo Life diorama pg. 18.)

- **Build a unique sculpture**

  Form a shape using newspaper, foil, foam, etc. Cover in Plaster Cloth and add unique details.

- **Make a three-dimensional picture**

  Build up the picture in three stages: background, middle ground and then foreground.

Casting Plaster

Casting Plaster has a wide variety of uses. Cast rocks, fossils, animal tracks and more. Use with a mold or natural impression. Easy to sand and paint.

Basic Use

1. Turn Casting Plaster container upside down and shake for 30 seconds. Add 2 tablespoons cold water into a clean bowl or mixing tray. Slowly add 6 level tablespoons of Casting Plaster into water.

2. Let stand for 2 minutes. Stir for at least 1 minute with a clean Stir Stick. Immediately pour Casting Plaster into mold. Plaster sets quickly, and is not pourable after 5 minutes.

3. Let casting set 40 minutes then remove from mold. Allow castings to dry 2-3 hours before coloring.

NOTES:

- Wash hands immediately after use.
- Clean wet Plaster out of mixing bowl right away or use a disposable bowl. Do NOT pour Plaster down drain; throw excess in trash.
- Mix only the amount of Casting Plaster needed for each project.
- Drying times will vary depending on heat and humidity.

- Rock Castings

- Prepare and use Casting Plaster per Basic Use instructions.
- Pour wet Plaster into a Rock Mold.
- To dislodge bubbles and level plaster, tap mold lightly.
- When set, twist mold to dislodge rock castings.
- Allow to dry 2 – 3 hours before coloring.
- Use the Leopard Spot paint technique to color rock castings. (See Paint pg. 160)

- various Styles and Shapes

Try these creative techniques to make unique rock shapes.

Fill Rock Mold 1/4 to 1/2 full of Casting Plaster.

Tilt Rock Mold in a variety of directions for different rock shapes.

Break rock casting into smaller pieces.

- Attach Rocks

- Test fit rocks on diorama.

- You may need to cut into terrain with a hobby knife for a good fit. This will not hurt the integrity of the Plaster Cloth terrain. It is very durable.

- Attach Rocks with Project Glue or Plaster Cloth.

 **or**

Project Glue

Apply Project Glue to backside of rock. Press in place at desired location. Hold until setting begins.

Plaster Cloth

Soak rock casting in water for 10 seconds. Spray or brush Plaster Cloth terrain with water (both surfaces need to be wet). Apply a small, wet wad of Plaster Cloth to backside of rock. Press in place at desired location.

- Blend Rocks

Plaster Cloth

- Cut small strips of Plaster Cloth (1" x 3").

- With a sponge, paintbrush or spray bottle, wet rock around the edges.

- Wet Plaster Cloth strip, place along edge of rock and poke in and around gaps. Do NOT get plaster on rock face or casting will lose its rock-like detail.

- Blend Cloth in with terrain as much as possible. Continue until gaps are filled.

Casting Plaster

- Prepare and use Casting Plaster per Basic Use instructions.

- Wet rock casting around the edges with a sponge, paintbrush or spray bottle.

- Using a Stir Stick, dab Casting Plaster around rock edges where there are gaps. Do NOT get plaster on rock face or casting will lose its rock-like detail.

- Create Textures

NOTE: Casting Plaster should be thinner than Basic Use instructions for these applications. Add a few drops of water at a time until consistency is slightly runny.

Smooth prepared Casting Plaster over damp Plaster Cloth to create a sleek finish.

Dab on to create natural terrain surfaces. (See Glaciers & Icebergs diorama pg. 14.)

Use Casting Plaster to seal a water area to prevent seepage of Realistic Water, and create a smooth river bottom. Pour along a modeled river to create silt deposits along edges of river bottom.

- More Casting Plaster Projects

Create Lava

- Prepare Casting Plaster per Basic Use instructions, adding an additional 1 teaspoon of water.
- Slowly pour wet Casting Plaster down the outside of a landscaped volcano, allowing "lava" to flow naturally.
- Let set 15 minutes. If desired, add second layer of lava.
- Paint to resemble look of lava. (See Paint pg. 162)

Cast Animal Tracks or Footprints

- Prepare and use Casting Plaster per Basic Use instructions.
- Slowly pour wet plaster into impression, level with the top.
- When set, carefully remove casting and brush off debris.
- Paint, if desired.

   TIP!
   When Casting Plaster is completely dry (approx. 12 hours), it can be washed to remove dirt.

Cast Household Items (Jewelry, Seashells, Action Figures, etc.)

- Press object into Sculpting Clay, making a clear impression. Carefully remove object.
- Prepare and use Casting Plaster per Basic Use instructions.
- Slowly pour plaster into clay impression, level with top.
- When set, carefully remove casting.
- Let dry, paint and decorate as desired.

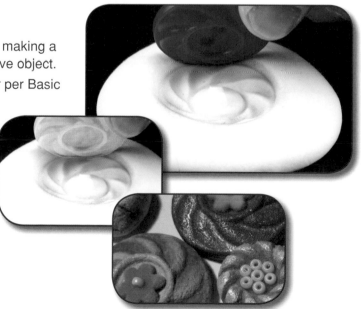

1

2

3

4

1. Create overgrowth and vines with Foliage Fiber. (See Foliage Fiber page 118)

2. Cast different size rocks or break them into smaller pieces to fit a desired landscape. (See Rock Castings page 10)

3. Model fallen trees using natural armature and sticks from nature. (See Trees page 127)

4. Stretch polyester fiberfill or cotton balls, glue to shoreline, then brush on Realistic Water. When nearly dry, stretch and shape splashes. Let dry, then repeat.

5. Model a shipwreck by attaching a cutaway portion of a toy boat, then fill in the surrounding area with crushed Talus.

6. Brush Realistic Water on Talus for a wet look.

7. Mix a small amount of white paint into Water Effects to model splashes along the shore. (See Water Effects page 132)

Landscape

ReadyGrass Sheets

ReadyGrass Sheets are the easy way to add flat, grassy areas or sandy surfaces to projects and dioramas. The turf is easy to remove to add roads, paths, water areas and more.

Available colors: Summer Grass, Green Grass, Desert Sand

Basic Use

Attach ReadyGrass Sheets with Sticky Bond using the Contact Gluing Method.

1. Use a Foam Brush to brush adhesive on Project Base (or other non-porous surface) and over entire back of ReadyGrass Sheet.

2. Brush glue out to all edges. Let dry until clear. Align ReadyGrass Sheet on surface and smooth to adhere.

3. Add landscape materials. (See Landscape pg. 116-135)

NOTES:
- Project Glue can be substituted with Sticky Bond for attaching ReadyGrass Sheets.
- When using the Backdrop with the Project Base, do not cover grooves in Base.
- ReadyGrass Sheets fit one large Project Base or two small Bases. When using a small Base, cut sheet in half widthwise.

– Remove Turf

Remove turf or sand to clear areas for paths, roads, water area, erosion and more.

- Using a pencil, draw outline of area.
- Using a Foam Brush, dab water inside the outline.
- Remove turf by scraping with handle of Foam Brush.
- Save turf scrapings for a later use.

– More ReadyGrass Uses

For water areas, run a continuous bead of Project Glue around perimeter of water area to contain Realistic Water. (See Realistic Water pg. 130)

Create a sandy sea floor and rocks using the Desert Sand ReadyGrass Sheet. (See Aquarium diorama pg. 10)

Using the Green Grass or Summer Grass sheet, design a park scene by scraping off turf, painting a lake, adding landscape and other fun details.

Get creative! Add newspaper wads under areas and design the Nile River with the Desert Sand Sheet. (See Life along the Nile diorama pg. 55)

Add moss and algae to water areas with turf scraped from ReadyGrass Sheet.

Add ReadyGrass to Backdrop to continue scene.

Ground Cover

Nature contains an endless number of grasses and plants growing in a variety of colors and heights. Ground cover begins with painting earth colors on rocks and terrain, and is followed by the application of Green Grass and other landscape materials.

Rock Colors

Rock castings are colored with Rock Colors pigments and the Leopard Spot painting technique. (See Leopard Spot pg. 160)

Earth Undercoat

Earth Undercoat is a liquid pigment designed to color Plaster Cloth. It provides natural-looking earth tones and highlights that model dirt and soil. The pigment also works on other materials, such as wood, foam and paper.

Basic Use

1. Brush diluted Earth Undercoat over Plaster Cloth terrain. (See Earth Undercoat pg. 171)

2. Let dry before adding landscape materials.

- **Paint Plaster Cloth Rocks**

- Make rocks and boulders from Plaster Cloth. Paint with diluted Earth Undercoat for a natural coloring.

- Dab on craft paint to add realistic earth tones.

Water Undercoat

Water Undercoat realistically colors water areas.
(See Paint Water Areas pg. 161)

Green Grass

Green Grass creates a natural grass covering on a terrain. Apply over Earth Undercoat.

Basic Use

1. Spray diluted Project Glue over terrain. Avoid rocks and water areas.
2. Sprinkle Green Grass over wet Glue.
3. Spray again with Project Glue to seal.

- Be Creative with Green Grass

Incorporate the terrain into your backdrop design by gluing Green Grass directly to the Backdrop.

Foliage Fiber

Foliage Fiber is a versatile material that can be used to create undergrowth, dense grass, foliage for trees, vines, hedges and more.

Basic Use

1. Separate thin layers of Foliage Fiber (approx. 5-7 layers).

2. Stretch until very thin and lacy (approx. twice its original size).

3. Place on terrain, spray with diluted Project Glue, sprinkle with Green Grass or Accent and spray again to seal. (See Project Glue pg. 170)

TIP! Trim stray strands of Foliage Fiber with scissors.

- Tree Foliage

Drape Tree Foliage over tree armatures for realistic looking trees. Use for a variation of height and color on a landscaped diorama.

- Stretch a layer of Foliage Fiber until very thin and lacy.
- Place on a paper towel or newspaper and spray with diluted Project Glue.
- Sprinkle with desired color of Accent. Let dry.
- Flip Foliage Fiber over and spray and sprinkle as above. Move to clean/dry newspaper. Let dry, then attach to an armature. (See Trees pg. 126)

- Puffy Tree Foliage

Attach Puffy Tree Foliage to terrain or make quick and easy puff ball trees.

- Tear off small pieces of Foliage Fiber. Pull in all directions until round and puffy.

- Spray with diluted Project Glue. Sprinkle with desired color(s) of Accent.

- Spray with diluted Project Glue to seal and let dry.

- Using Project Glue, attach to natural armatures or terrain.

- Make Vines

- Separate a thin section of stretched Foliage Fiber.

- Form or pull into vine shape.

- Sprinkle with desired color of Accent and Flowers.

- Spray with diluted Project Glue.

- When dry, glue in place with Project Glue.

- Make Hedges

- Cut a section of Foliage Fiber.

- Spray with diluted Project Glue, sprinkle with Flowers or an Accent.

- Glue in place with Project Glue.

Shrubs and Bushes

Create medium height ground cover with Shrubs and Bushes.

Basic Use

1. Apply Project Glue where you want Shrubs or Bushes.
2. Press Shrubs or Bushes into Glue.

– Placing Shrubs and Bushes

Sprinkle desired color of Accent or Flowers on Shrubs and Bushes for natural color variations. (See Accents pg. 121)

Shrubs and bushes look natural when placed in groups.

Place around rocks and along hillsides.

Blend trees into landscape by placing Shrubs or Bushes around bases.

Place along edges of buildings to hide gaps between terrain and building.

Make three-dimensional trees by gluing Shrubs to the Backdrop. Paint trunks with Project Paints.

Accents

Add realistic textures and highlights to grasses, Shrubs, Bushes, Foliage Fiber, vines, trees and more.

Basic Use

1. Spray diluted Project Glue where you want Accents. (See Project Glue pg. 170)

2. Sprinkle desired color of Accent.

3. Spray again with Project Glue to seal.

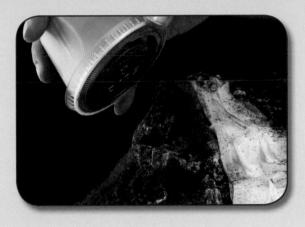

- Where to Add Accents

Create a path by sprinkling darker colors of Accents.

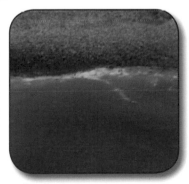

Apply dark green Accents around water areas where the ground is well-watered.

Sprinkle on stretched Foliage Fiber to add color and texture.

Wild Grass

Create tall ground cover with Wild Grass.

Basic Use

1. Remove a pinch of Wild Grass, then roll between fingers for an uneven, natural look.

2. Cut to preferred length with scissors.

3. Dip cut end in Project Glue and place on diorama. Hold until setting begins.

- Where to Use Wild Grass

Create a wheat field.

Add natural grasses to a landscape.

Add a thatch roof to a structure. Tie together for thatch bundles.

Flowers

Add flowers and highlights to landscape, such as grasses, Shrubs, Foliage Fiber, hedges, vines and trees.

Basic Use

1. Spray diluted Project Glue where you want Flowers. (See Project Glue pg. 170)

2. Sprinkle Flowers over wet Glue.

3. Spray again with Project Glue to seal.

- Where to Use Flowers

A very light dusting of Yellow Flowers creates a sun drenched look.

Brush tips of a Desert Plant in Project Glue, then dip in Red or Yellow Flowers.

Create flowering foliage by sprinkling Red or Yellow Flowers over stretched Foliage Fiber.

Talus

Talus (rock debris) is part of the natural erosion process and is found in many places, including the base of mountains and near rock cuts, and along rivers and streams.

Basic Use

1. Apply Project Glue on rock debris area.

2. Press Talus into wet Glue.

- Small Rocks and Sand

Crush Talus for a variety of rock sizes or crush into sand. A mixture of sand and larger pieces provides a realistic effect.

- Place Talus in a plastic bag and seal.

- On a safe surface, tap with a hammer until desired size is achieved.

- Spray desired area with diluted Project Glue, sprinkle crushed Talus over wet Glue, then spray Glue again to seal.

- Color Talus

Color Talus to blend with terrain.

- In a disposable cup, add Talus to Earth Undercoat, Rock Colors, Project Paint or craft paint. The more diluted the paint, the lighter the Talus will be.

- Mix Talus and paint thoroughly with a Stir Stick. Let set until desired color is achieved.

- Let dry on newspaper.

- If Talus is too dark, spray with water to lighten.

- Attach to diorama with diluted Project Glue.

Model rocks in water.

Line a road with Talus.
Create a gravel path.

Form a fire pit.

White Fiber

Add clouds to a diorama or create smoke to intensify a volcanic eruption.

Basic Use

1. Cut a piece of White Fiber.
2. Pull in all directions until fluffy and cloud-like.
3. Attach to Backdrop with Project Glue.

TIP! You can substitute cotton balls or polyester fiberfill for White Fiber.

- Smoke

- Remove a portion of White Fiber, then pull and twist into smoke-like shape.
- Dab with gray paint.
- Glue to firewood in a fire pit or around the rim of a volcano.

Trees

Trees are a great way to add a realistic touch to any landscape.

Deciduous Trees

Bendable plastic Tree Armatures retain their shape.

Basic Use

1. Bend and twist Tree Armature into a realistic, three-dimensional shape.

2. Brush Sticky Bond on "leaf" area of branches. Avoid trunk where foliage does not naturally grow.

3. Place Armature in the optional base. Let Sticky Bond dry until clear and tacky.

4. Firmly press Shrubs or Bushes onto branches.

5. Spray with diluted Project Glue to seal. (See Project Glue pg. 170)

6. Let dry, then plant on diorama. (See Plant Trees pg. 128)

Deciduous Trees Using Natural Armatures

Natural armatures are plant clippings that resemble trees. Use tree-shaped twigs, flower stems and trimmings of shrubs or hedges. The possibilities are endless!

Basic Use

1. Prepare Tree Foliage. (See Tree Foliage pg. 118)

2. Brush Sticky Bond on "leaf" area. Let dry until clear and tacky.

3. Drape branches with Tree Foliage.

4. Spray with diluted Project Glue to seal. (See Project Glue pg. 170)

Conifer Trees

Conifers can be created from Foliage Fiber or clippings from living evergreens.

Basic Use

1. Cut a piece of Foliage Fiber into a triangular shape.

2. Stretch and twist into a conifer tree shape.

3. Spray with diluted Project Glue. (See Project Glue pg. 170)

4. Sprinkle desired color(s) of Accent.

5. Spray again with diluted Project Glue to seal.

6. Cut bottom of tree flat, then attach to diorama with Project Glue.

– Evergreen Clippings

- Cut a small section of evergreen plant. Spray clipping with diluted Project Glue.
- Sprinkle with desired color(s) of Accent.
- Spray again with diluted Project Glue.
- See Plant Trees below.

– Get Creative with Trees

Cut Tree Armatures into smaller trees and bushes.

Attach Tree Foliage to Tree Armatures.

Use tree-shaped twigs with no foliage to model dead trees.

Plant Trees

Use Project Glue to plant trees.

Basic Use

1. Place Tree Armature into optional base.
2. Place base on diorama or glue in place using Project Glue.

– Permanent Placement

Poke a small hole into terrain with a hobby knife.

Cover hole with a large drop of Project Glue.

Push base pin (Tree Armatures) or base of tree (natural armatures) into hole.

– More Ideas

Glue Shrubs around the base of tree to blend with landscape.

Cut stem on natural armature at an angle for easy planting.

Plant smaller trees near the back and larger trees in front to enhance the perspective of distance.

Desert Plants

Create an authentic desert scene with prickly pears and saguaro, barrel and columnar cacti.

Basic Use

1. Remove Desert Plants from sprue, then sand lightly to remove excess plastic.

2. Columnar and Prickly Pear: Use Project Glue to attach cacti to bases.

3. Let dry, then plant on diorama using Project Glue.

- Paint Plants

- Paint Desert Plants to change their look.

- Paint with acrylic paint. Or add a tiny amount of Project Glue to tempera paint. The glue keeps tempera paint from peeling off plastic.

Water Areas

Create realistic water areas, such as lakes, ponds, rivers, waterfalls and more.

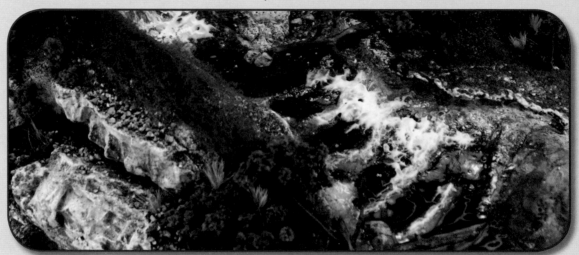

Realistic Water

Realistic Water dries clear and the reflective surface gives the illusion of depth. Use it to model rivers, ponds, lakes and more.

Basic Use

Do NOT shake bottle of Realistic Water. This will create unwanted bubbles.

1. Prepare water area. (See Paint Water Areas page 161)

2. Pour Realistic Water slowly onto prepared water area. Pour no deeper than 1/8". If water area is deeper than 1/8", dry 24 hours between 1/8" layers.

3. Pull out to edges with a Stir Stick, toothpick or tip of Foam Brush.

– Submerge Items

- Use a tiny bit of Project Glue to attach items such as dried twigs and Talus around a water area.

- Let glue dry completely, then pour Realistic Water.

NOTE: An excessive amount of glue will temporarily turn Realistic Water cloudy. Eventually, it will clear.

– Ripples

- Using a squeeze bottle, pool desired amount of Realistic Water onto slick side of Release Paper (freezer paper).

- When dry (approx. 24 hours), use the squeeze bottle to apply additional Realistic Water on top of pool in a swirl pattern. Let dry.

- Use a spatula to remove ripple from release paper. Apply a small amount of Realistic Water on back of ripple and place where desired.

– Water Area Ideas

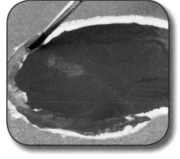

Run a continuous bead of Project Glue around the perimeter of a water area to contain Realistic Water. Let Project Glue dry before pouring Realistic Water.

When painting a water area, use dark paint colors to model deep water and light colors to model shallow areas near the shoreline. (See Paint pg. 161)

Model a swamp area with Realistic Water, Wild Grass and twigs.

- Shiny Areas

- Brush Realistic Water over a completed project to give it a wet (shiny) appearance.
- Brush Realistic Water on painted rock castings to give the appearance of water seeping through the rock.

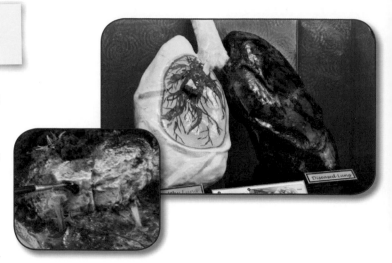

Water Effects

Water Effects is moldable and will hold its shape to create water splashes, white caps, waterfalls and icicles.

Basic Use

1. Dab Water Effects on top of dried Realistic Water with a Stir Stick to create desired effect.
2. Let dry until clear (approximately 24 hours).

- White Caps

- Mix a small amount of white Project Paint (or acrylic paint) with Water Effects.
- Dab on with a Stir Stick to create a white cap effect.

- Waterfalls

- Determine the length and width of waterfall and add 1/2" to length (for attaching waterfall when dry). Using a Stir Stick or toothpick, apply Water Effects on the slick side of Release Paper (freezer paper or non-stick pan).

- Feather the ends with a Stir Stick or toothpick.

- Allow to dry until clear. Peel dried Water Effects from Release Paper.

- Apply a small amount of Water Effects to underside of waterfall ends and press in place.

- When in place, apply a small amount of Water Effects at ends of waterfall to add texture and blend into the natural flow of water.

- Icicles

- Spread a line of Water Effects onto slick side of Release Paper (freezer paper or non-stick pan).

- To shape icicles, pull through Water Effects with a Stir Stick or toothpick. Allow to dry until clear.

- Attach by applying Water Effects on backside of icicles, then press in place.

TIP! Mix a small amount of glitter into Water Effects before making icicles. The glitter will make your icicles sparkle!

- Fountains

Create a flowing fountain with Water Effects.

- Dab Water Effects on standing water areas.

- For falling water, dab Water Effects on Release paper in desired length and shape. Let dry until clear and attach with Water Effects.

Snow

Make a snow scene! Add glaciers, icebergs or a heavy snow cover to a diorama or display.

Snow Areas

It's easy to change a diorama into a snow scene.

Basic Use

1. Paint area with Snow Base.
2. Sprinkle with Snowflakes while Snow Base is wet.
3. Spray with diluted Project Glue to seal. (See Project Glue pg. 170)

- Snow Mixture

Add snowdrifts or a heavy snow cover to a diorama.

- Mix equal amounts of Snow Base and Snowflakes.
- Spread mixture with a Stir Stick.
- Sprinkle with additional Snowflakes while mixture is wet.

NOTE: The amount of Snowflakes mixed into snow mixture will change its density.

– Light Snow Dusting

Give trees and ground cover a very light dusting of snow.

- Spray area with diluted Project Glue.
- Sprinkle Snowflakes while glue is wet.
- Spray with diluted Project Glue to seal. (See Project Glue pg. 170)

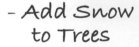

– Backdrop Snow

Make your backdrop scene three-dimensional with Backdrop Snow.

- Mix equal amounts of Project Glue and Snow Base.
- Slowly mix in Snowflakes until desired consistency has been achieved.
- Dab snow mixture on desired location.
- Sprinkle additional Snowflakes on top of wet snow mixture.

– Make a Frozen Pond

Create a realistic snow covered pond.

- Prepare and paint a water area. (See Water Areas pg. 161)
- Pour Realistic Water slowly onto dried water area.
- While Realistic Water is wet, lightly sprinkle Snowflakes.
- Let dry 24 hours.

– Add Snow to Trees

- Dab Snow Mixture on trees, working from top to bottom. Sprinkle with Snowflakes while mixture is wet.
- Sprinkle additional Snowflakes on tree while Snow Mixture is wet.

TIP! When painting glaciers, dab light blue Project Paint randomly over Snow Base for a more "icy" look.

- Make It Real

1. Use a variety of ground cover materials for a realistic landscape. (See Ground Cover page 116-125)

2. Crush and color Talus to match the region you are modeling. (See Talus page 123)

3. Model a flowing river by adding strips of Plaster Cloth to the river bottom. (See Flowing River page 106)

4. To add even more realism to your diorama, use a photo of an actual landscape as the backdrop.

5. Add a variety of tree types to model a realistic forest.

6. Place Shrubs and Bushes around the base of trees to add a realistic touch.

7. Create river debris using Woodland Scenics Deadfall (S30) and Talus (C1270 - C1285).

Sculpt

Sculpting Clay

Sculpting Clay is air-dry modeling clay. It is easy to cut, sand and color. Use Sculpting Clay to sculpt figures, plants and animals for dioramas and displays, add details to masks and buildings, model a cell, do a fun craft and much, much more.

Basic Use

1. Use Sculpting Clay on a clean, flat surface.
2. Sculpt using clean hands and materials.
3. Take only the amount of Clay you need and **keep unused portion in closed package.**
4. Sculpting Clay must be conditioned before you begin sculpting. To condition Clay, roll into a ball shape, then into a rope shape and back into a ball shape.

5. Begin Sculpting. Sculpt on a piece of wax paper so pieces are easy to remove. Fresh Sculpting Clay will stick to itself by pressing or pinching pieces together. Or, attach dry pieces together with Project Glue.

6. Dip Sculpting Tool or fingers in water and smooth over connection points to blend fresh pieces together.

7. After sculpture is complete, allow Clay to dry approximately 24 hours. For thick pieces, turn over while drying so all sides are exposed to air.

8. When Clay has dried, sand any rough areas lightly with 220 grit (fine grade) sandpaper.

9. Dried Clay can be colored with Project Paint, craft paint or markers.

10. Store remaining Clay in a sealable plastic bag. Conditioned Clay is easier to work with.

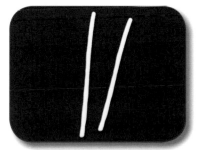

- Basic Techniques

Sculpting Clay figures are typically sculpted in parts. Parts are sculpted individually, then attached together to form a complete figure. (See Basic Use instructions page 138 before beginning)

• Flatten Sculpting Clay by hand or with a rolling pin.

• Begin all shapes as a ball. This allows you to easily smooth the Clay surface.

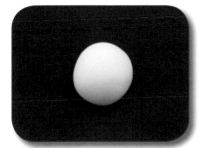

Ball: Remove desired amount of Clay. Roll Clay between palms until surface of Clay is smooth.

Cone: Start with a ball shape, then place hands into a "V" and roll Clay in a back-and-forth motion.

Rope: Place hands together over ball shape and move back and forth, slowly moving hands outward. Apply even pressure and don't press too hard.

Tube: Flatten Clay, roll around a pencil or dowel, then remove. Use for sculpting hollow objects like pipes, a hollowed out log, pant legs and more.

Pinch: Pinch Clay to form fins, tails, noses, necks and more.

Sculpting Tool: Use Sculpting Tool to indent features (eyes, nose, ears, etc.), add details (scribe textures for wood, feathers, brick and stone patterns, etc.), poke holes and cut while Clay is fresh.

- Measure Clay

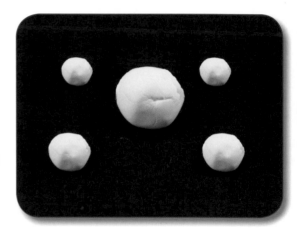

- Clay is measured in balls. This ensures what you are sculpting is proportionally correct.
- As an example, roll a ball of Clay for torso and a smaller ball for the head, equal size balls for legs, ears, etc.
- When rolling balls (all at the same time) store in plastic bag until ready to use.

TIPS!

- The Scene-A-Rama Sculpting Kit includes a double-ended Sculpting Tool. This versatile tool is designed to cut fresh or dried Clay, add details to a sculpture, poke holes, draw lines and more.

- Smooth away creases in sculpture with wet fingers.

- If pieces are drying too quickly, rub a drop of water over surface of Clay.

- If sculpted pieces are too soft to work with, let set a while between construction steps.

- If your sculpture is not working out as you would like, start again. We do it all the time!

Sculpt Figures, Plants & Animals

See Basic Use instructions pg. 138 before beginning.

- Sculpt a Figure

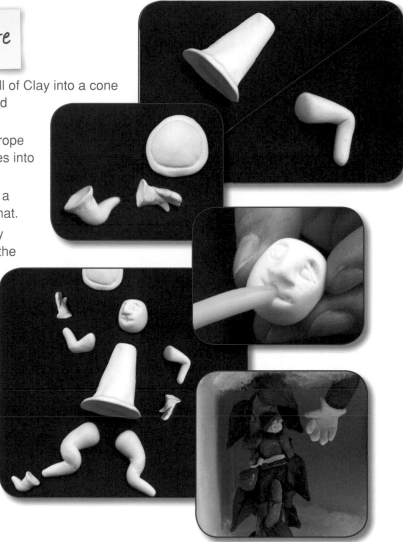

- For the body, form a ball of Clay into a cone shape, then pinch to add detail to bottom of shirt.
- Form balls of Clay into rope shapes. Shape the ropes into arms, legs and feet.
- Form a ball of Clay into a concave shape for the hat.
- Form small balls of Clay into hand shapes. Use the Sculpting Tools to add fingers and other details.
- Form a ball of Clay into a head shape. Use the Sculpting Tool to add facial details.
- Assemble figure with Project Glue.
- Let dry, then paint.

- Sculpt a Whale

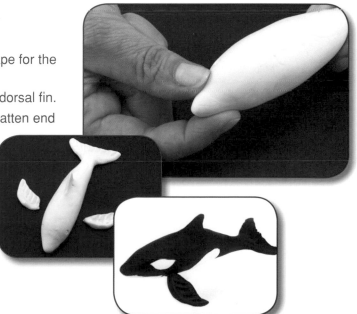

- Form ball of Clay into a cone shape for the body.
- Pinch Clay to form the nose and dorsal fin.
- Pinch to elongate the body and flatten end for tail.
- Use Sculpting Tool to carve tail. Flatten again at end.
- Carve area for mouth and poke to form eyes.
- Flatten a small ball of Clay and cut out flippers with Sculpting Tool.
- Attach flippers with Project Glue.
- Let dry, then paint.

- Sculpt a Sea Star

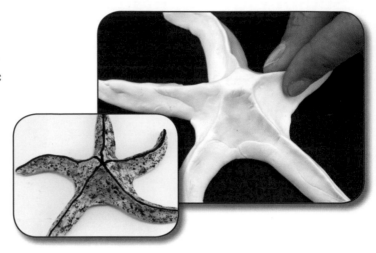

- Form Sculpting Clay into basic sea star shape.
- Pinch to add detail.
- Let dry, then paint.

- Sculpt Coral

- Roll a desired number of elongated cone shapes. Flatten bottom for gluing.
- Using tip of Sculpting Tool, mark a crisscross shape on top. Pinch to add detail.
- Let dry, then glue together with Project Glue.
- Form a piece of Clay into a circle shape, let dry, then paint. (Base for coral)
- Glue coral to base, let dry and paint coral as desired.

- Sculpt Sea Plants

- Flatten Clay (approx. 1/8" thick) with a rolling pin.
- Using the Sculpting Tool, draw leaf shapes in Clay. Let set for a minute or two, then cut apart. Add leaf pattern.
- For curved shape, place leaves on dowels while drying.
- Paint when dry.
- Form a piece of Clay into a circle shape, let dry, then paint. (Base for sea plants)
- Glue leaves to base.

- Sculpt a Flower

- Flatten Clay (approx. 1/8" thick) with a rolling pin.
- Using the Sculpting Tool, cut out petal shapes and add details.
- Assemble petals with Project Glue.
- Roll tiny dots of Clay and glue to center of flower. Add details with blunt end of Sculpting Tool.
- Let dry, then paint.

Sculpt Buildings & Add Textures

- Clay Structure

- Flatten Clay (approx. 1/8" thick) between two sheets of wax paper with a rolling pin.
- Use a ruler or Sculpting Tool to cut walls. Use Sculpting Tool to cut out windows, doors, shutters, etc. Store Clay cutouts between two sheets of wax paper or in a plastic bag to keep them from drying out too quickly.
- To create window or door coverings, flatten window and door cutouts slightly larger than window and door openings in walls.
- Add a texture to walls, windows or doors. (See texture Walls below)
- Glue windows and doors to backside of wall with Project Glue. Next, glue walls together and attach roof. (See Shingle Roof page 144)
- Let dry, then paint. (See Painting Techniques pg. 158-159)

- Texture Walls

Use the Sculpting Tool to add a brick, stone or log pattern to fresh Clay.

- Shutters, Doors & Gates

- Roll Clay flat (approx. 1/16") and cut strips to desired height.
- Use the Sculpting Tool to mark lines for planks, then score Clay for a wood grain effect.
- Let dry, and paint as desired.
- Attach using Project Glue.

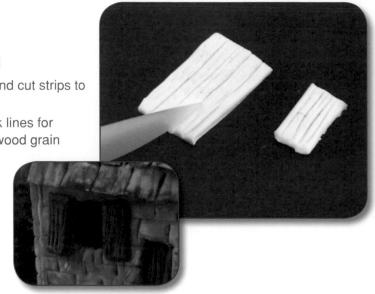

- Shingle Roof

- Determine size of roof. Cut out of Construction Board.
- Flatten Clay (approx. 1/16" thick). Using the Sculpting Tool, cut strips of Clay the length of roof.
- Make vertical cuts equal distance apart.
- Glue shingles to roof. Start at the bottom and overlap each layer. Work toward the top on each side.
- Cut a strip twice the width of the others, and make horizontal cuts on both sides. Fold over the peak of the roof for the final layer. Glue in place.

- More Ideas

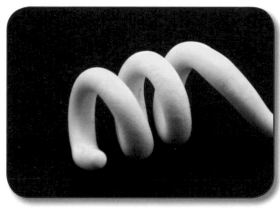

Form Clay around Project Wire, a pipe cleaner or foil to add stability to a sculpture or create a unique shape.

Give your project a shiny finish by brushing on Realistic Water.

Brush on diluted Project Glue and sprinkle with glitter.

Add texture to Clay by pressing a screen, leaf, teeth of a comb, toothpick, cloth, etc. into fresh Clay.

Decorate sculpted pieces with embellishments, like buttons, beads, seashells, feathers, yarn, etc. Press on while Clay is damp or attach with Project Glue.

Hang a flat sculpture. Embed a paper clip in back of damp Clay and let dry. Secure with Project Glue.

Fun Fur

Fun Fur is fun! It is a great way to add animal fur, hair or other such effects to a project.

Basic Use

1. Brush diluted Project Glue (pg. 170) where you would like Fun Fur.

2. Sprinkle Fun Fur over glue.

3. Let dry.

TIP! Shake excess Fun Fur over a paper towel so you can save it for another use.

— Where to use Fun Fur

Add fur to an animal sculpture.

Model a teddy bear or add head and facial hair to a mask.

Add elements to a diorama, like a seal skin blanket.

Buildings & Structures

Basic Structure

Basic Use

Walls, Windows and Doors

1. Using a pencil and ruler, draw structure pattern (including windows and doors) on Project Board.

2. Add a pattern or texture, if desired. (See Patterns & Textures page 152)

3. Using a hobby knife, cut out walls, windows and doors. Add special details, if desired. (See Structure Details page 149)

Assemble Walls

1. Using the Contact Gluing Method (pg. 169), assemble walls.

2. Begin by applying Project Glue along the front edge of a side wall. Press front wall and side wall in place. Let dry.

3. Repeat with opposite side wall. Let dry.

4. Glue front wall assembly to back wall. Let dry.

Roof

1. Draw roof on Project Board and cut out with hobby knife. The roof should extend slightly over each of the four walls, creating an overhang. If you need help in determining the proper size of roof, make a sample roof from scratch paper. When the proper size has been determined, trace sample roof on Project Board.

2. Add shingles to roof, if desired. (See Shingles page 150)

3. Mark centerline on underside of roof for peak. Score along centerline mark by indenting with the dull end of a paintbrush. Bend roof to form pitched roof.

4. Using the Contact Gluing Method (pg. 169), attach roof. Let dry.

5. Paint structure as desired. (See Painting Techniques page 158-159)

TIP! The Scene-A-Rama Building & Structure Kit (SP4130) has all the materials you need to create your own unique structures.

Structure Details

Use these details to personalize your structure.

Hinged Doors and Shutters

Hinged doors and shutters add a realistic touch.

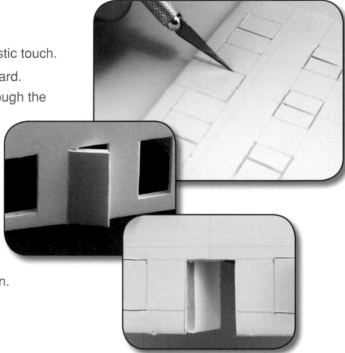

- Draw door/windows on Project Board.
- Cut three (3) sides all the way through the Project Board.
- On the fourth side, cut the top layer of paper and foam only. The uncut paper layer acts as a hinge.
- **Out-swing:** Make the fourth cut on the backside. Gently push open.
- **In-swing:** Make the fourth cut on the front side. Gently push open.

Window Treatments

Use clear plastic to add windows treatments.

- Measure and mark window openings, adding 1/8" on all sides.
- Use paint or permanent markers to add a window design, if desired.
- Cut out windows with scissors or hobby knife.
- Attach to backside of wall with Project Glue or tape.

NOTE: If a window design was added, make sure it faces the inside of the structure.

- Shingles

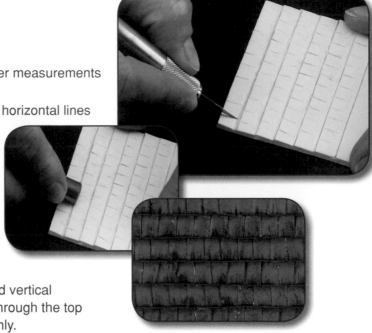

- Determine size of roof. Transfer measurements to Project Board, then cut out.
- Using a pencil and ruler, draw horizontal lines on Project Board. Shingles are usually taller than they are wide.
- Draw vertical lines in an alternating pattern between horizontal lines. The spacing between the vertical lines will be the width of the shingles.
- Score by cutting horizontal and vertical lines with a hobby knife. Cut through the top layer of paper and the foam only.
- Push down at an angle along the top of each horizontal line with the end of a ruler to shape the shingle. Start at the peak and work down on each side of the roof.
- Holding the ruler at an angle, push in at each vertical line.
- Paint shingles in desired color, then highlight with the Drybrush paint technique. (See Paint Shingles page 158)

- Spanish Tile Roof

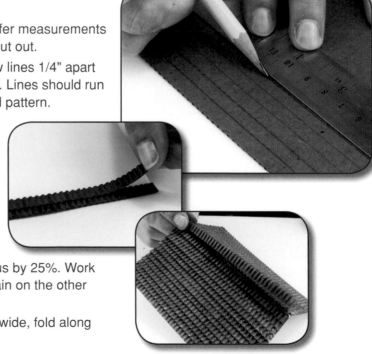

- Determine size of roof. Transfer measurements to Construction Board, then cut out.
- Using a pencil and ruler, draw lines 1/4" apart on backside of Ribbed Board. Lines should run in opposite direction of ribbed pattern.
- Paint front of Ribbed Board with a terra-cotta paint color and let dry. (See Mixing Unique Colors page 157)
- Cut out strips with scissors or hobby knife.
- Starting at the bottom of the Construction Board, glue strips overlapping the previous by 25%. Work up to the peak, then start again on the other side.
- For the peak, cut a strip 1/2" wide, fold along centerline and glue in place.

- Occupied Structure

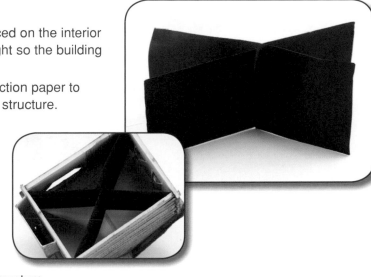

- Black construction paper placed on the interior of a structure will block the light so the building looks occupied.
- Cut 2 sheets of black construction paper to height and width of interior of structure.

  NOTE: Measure width of structure diagonally.

- Lay the two sheets on top of each other.
- Mark centerline, and cut a notch halfway up sheet.
- Assemble paper creating an "X".
- Insert paper diagonally into structure.
- Place a drop of glue on all corners to hold black paper in place.

Patterns & Textures

- Brick Pattern

The size of your brick pattern should be in proportion to your structure.

- Using a fine tip permanent marker and ruler, draw horizontal lines on Construction Board. The spacing between the lines will represent the height of your brick.
- Along bottom of wall, mark vertical lines for width of brick. Bricks are usually wider than they are tall.
- Using the mark as a gauge, draw vertical lines on every other row.
- Draw additional vertical lines halfway between marks on alternate rows.

Painting Suggestion: Choose a paint technique that shows off the brick pattern and does not hide it. Try the Stippling technique or Color Wash (pg.158).

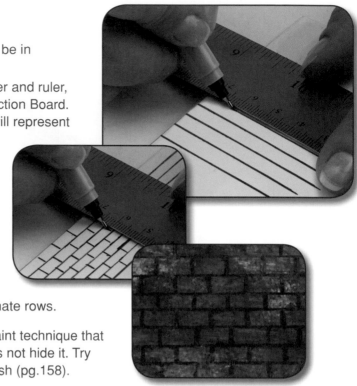

- Brick on a Round Structure

- Draw brick pattern as noted above on Project Board.
- Score by cutting brick pattern with a hobby knife. Cut through the top layer of paper and the foam only.
- Roll piece together.
- Apply glue along seam.
- Hold with rubber bands while drying.

Painting Suggestion: Use two or three different colors and the Stippling paint technique (pg. 158).

- Stone Pattern

- Using a pencil, draw a stone-shape pattern. The pencil markings represent cement or mortar. Use this technique on Project Board, Construction Board or a ReadyGrass Sheet.

OPTION: Make indentations into Project Board by pressing with a blunt instrument.

Painting Suggestion: A Color Wash allows the stone pattern to remain visible through the paint.

- Lap Siding

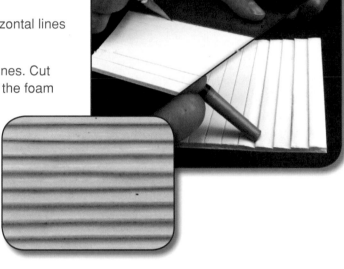

- Using a pencil and ruler, draw horizontal lines on Project Board.

- Score by cutting along horizontal lines. Cut through the top layer of paper and the foam only.

- Push down at an angle along top of score marks with the end of a ruler.

Painting Suggestion: Paint the lap siding with horizontal brush strokes.

- Log Pattern

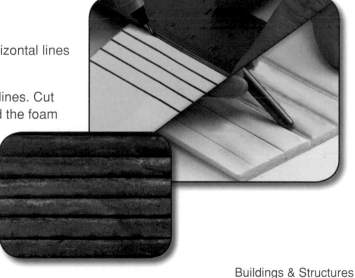

- Using a pencil and ruler, draw horizontal lines on Project Board.

- Score by cutting along horizontal lines. Cut through the top layer of paper and the foam only.

- Using the dull end of a paintbrush, indent along score lines.

Painting Suggestion: Make sure to get the paint into all the crevices in the log pattern.

- Corrugated Metal

- Using a pencil and ruler, draw structure pattern (including windows and doors) on backside of Ribbed Board. Make sure the lines of the Ribbed Board are vertical.

- Cut out with scissors or hobby knife.

- Glue Ribbed Board to Project Board structure.

Painting Suggestion: A silver metallic paint color models actual corrugated metal.

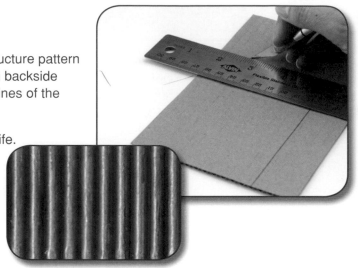

Assembly Techniques

- Basic Technique

- Begin by applying Project Glue along the front edge of a side wall. Press front wall and side wall in place. Let dry.

- Repeat with opposite side wall. Let dry.

- Glue front wall assembly to back wall. Let dry.

- Notch Technique

- Along inside edge of the front wall and back wall, measure and mark 1/8" from edge.

- Score by cutting along the mark through top layer of paper and foam only.

- From side, cut out foam and top layer of paper, then remove.

- Apply glue along notch, then assemble walls. Make sure walls are square.

- Let dry, then paint.

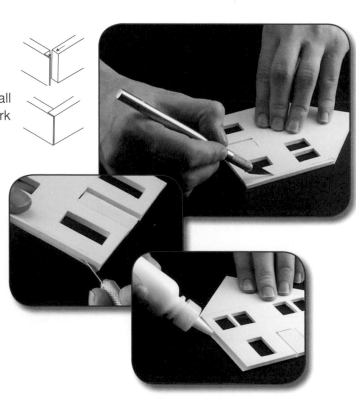

- Miter Technique

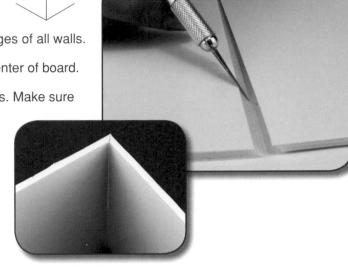

- Cut 45° angles along inside edges of all walls.

- Angles should be cut toward center of board.

- Apply glue, then assemble walls. Make sure walls are square.

- Let dry, then paint.

- Adjoining Walls

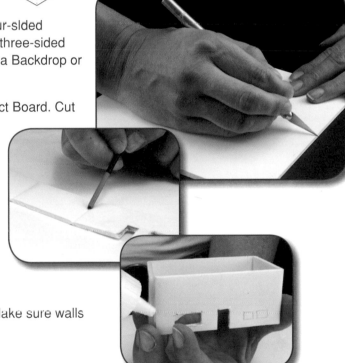

Use this technique to easily create four-sided structures. It is also great for two and three-sided structures that are placed up against, a Backdrop or terrain.

- Draw walls as one piece on Project Board. Cut out with hobby knife.

- Mark walls at desired bend points.

- Score along bend point on inside of wall by indenting with the dull end of a paintbrush.

- Bend Project Board inward at score line to form wall shape.

- Install walls using Project Glue. Make sure walls are square.

- Let dry, then paint.

Paint

Project Paints

Simple painting techniques add amazing results to school projects and dioramas.

Basic Use

1. Project Paints are concentrated. Dip paintbrush in water frequently while painting. This will extend the paint and allow it to spread more smoothly.

2. When switching colors, rinse brush thoroughly and blot on a paper towel. Do not let brush sit in water.

3. After use, wash paintbrushes in warm, soapy water and rinse well.

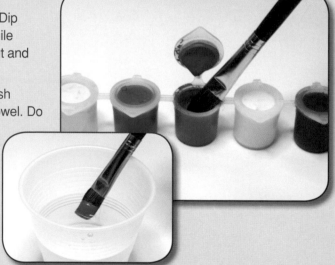

- Color Mixing Suggestions

When creating paint colors, always start with the lighter color first. Mix a very small amount of the darker paint color into the lighter until the desired color is achieved.

Mixing Primary Colors (Red, Blue & Yellow)

Yellow + Blue = Green   Yellow + Red = Orange   Red + Blue = Purple

Mixing Primary and Secondary Colors (Green, Orange & Purple)

Yellow + Green = Lime Green   Green + Blue = Aquamarine   Blue + Purple = Violet

Red + Purple = Plum   Orange + Red = Burnt Orange   Yellow + Orange = Tangerine

Mixing Landscape Colors

Green + Red + touch of Black = Forest Green   Yellow + Red + touch of Black = Brown   White + touch of Blue = Sky Blue

Mixing Unique Colors

Red + Yellow + touch of Brown = Terra-Cotta   White + touch of Blue + touch of Black = Steel Blue   White + touch of Yellow + touch of Black = Stone

TIPS!

- Mix 2-3 drops of white to lighten a color.
- Mix a tiny amount of black to darken a color.
- When creating unique colors, mix no more than two secondary colors together. Otherwise, colors become muted and dull.

Painting Techniques

Test paint techniques that are new to you on scrap material before painting your project.

- Color Wash

This technique is great for highlighting details. Use a black or dark gray wash for best results.

- Dip paintbrush in a Color Wash (pg. 171).
- Brush paint over entire structure or on a desired area.
- Continue until desired look is achieved.

- Drybrushing

This technique is great for weathering a structure. Apply over a painted surface.

- Dip paintbrush tip in a small amount of paint.
- Brush on a paper towel until nearly clean of paint.
- Brush on desired location.
- Continue until desired look is achieved.

- Stippling

A stiff-bristle paintbrush is recommended for this technique.

- Dip tips of bristles in paint.
- Dab brush on surface repeatedly.
- Apply paint in layers until desired look is achieved.

– Texturing (Bubble Effect)

This technique is great fun for everyone!

- Mix a few drops of liquid soap with water until bubbly.
- Dip paintbrush tip in a small amount of paint.
- Then, drag paintbrush along the soapy mixture, picking up bubbles.
- Brush on surface in a circular motion. Add more bubbles, if desired.
- Continue until desired look is achieved.
- Let bubbles pop naturally as paint dries.

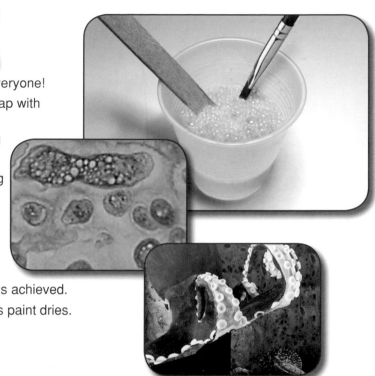

– Sponging

This technique is great for painting clouds or a forest full of trees.

- Cut a small piece of household sponge.
- Dip in a small amount of paint.
- Lightly dab on surface repeatedly, making a textured pattern.
- Continue until desired look is achieved.

– Blending

Blend colors together to create a unique look.

- Paint an object with a color.
- While paint is wet, add another color. Do not rinse brush between colors.
- Blend and dab colors together with a wet paintbrush.

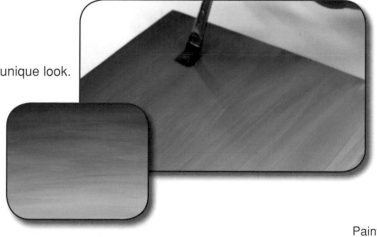

- Rinse Water

This technique is great for staining wood Project Sticks.

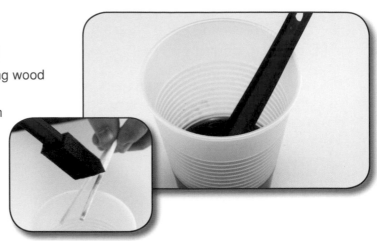

- Use the water that has been used to rinse a paintbrush while painting.

- Water should have a mix of many colors and be a dirty brown color.

- Brush on like a stain.

- Leopard Spot

Use the Leopard Spot paint technique to realistically color rock castings. Let colors run together naturally. Rinse brush between steps.

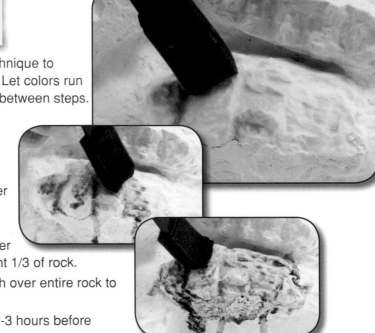

- Dilute Rock Colors with water. (See Rock Colors pg. 171)

- Using a Foam Brush, randomly dab Yellow Ocher Color Wash over 1/3 of rock.

- Randomly dab Burnt Umber Color Wash over a different 1/3 of rock.

- Brush and dab Black Wash over entire rock to tie colors together.

NOTE: Let rock castings dry 2-3 hours before coloring

- Paint Water Areas

Use this technique on Plaster Cloth terrain (See Plaster Cloth **TIPS!** pg. 105) or ReadyGrass Sheet (See Remove Turf pg. 115). Dark paint colors model deep water, while light colors model shallow.

- Paint water area with Water Undercoat or dark blue acrylic paint.

- Paint center of water area only. Do NOT paint area along edge of shoreline.

- Dip paintbrush in water, then dab brush along edge of WET paint, pulling it toward the shoreline. The paint will naturally follow the flow of the water. The lighter paint color will model the shallow shoreline.

- Let paint dry completely, then add Realistic Water (See Realistic Water pg. 130)

- Paint Lava

- Dilute black paint (1-part paint to 1-part water) and brush onto "lava flow."
- Paint in layers until desired color and effect is achieved.
- Model the high temperature of lava by dabbing on small amounts of red and yellow paint around edges of lava flow in various locations. Then, using a wet brush, gently blend colors together. Do not create a solid orange color, let colors naturally mix together. There should be some areas of yellow, some areas of red and some areas of orange.

- Paint Shingles

- Brush and dab paint on shingles, getting it into all the cracks and crevices.
- Use downward brush strokes to create natural looking shingles. Let dry.
- Highlight shingles with black paint and the Drybrush paint technique (pg.158).

- Paint Spanish Tile Roof

- See Spanish Tile Roof (pg. 150) for instructions on constructing roof.
- See Terra Cotta paint color. (pg. 157). Experiment with different amounts of paint to achieve desired terra cotta color.
- After roof is assembled, apply a black Color Wash. (pg. 171). Let the wash flow naturally into the roof crevices.

Paint Landscape

Use these simple painting techniques to enhance a landscape scene on your Backdrop. Practice these techniques on scratch material before painting your actual Backdrop.

Flat Paintbrush

Round Paintbrush

– Paint Deciduous Trees

- Using a small, round paintbrush, paint tree trunk and limbs. Dip brush in paint and water as needed.
- Using a fine tip, round paintbrush, apply black paint along trunk and limbs in thin strokes to create shadows.
- Cut a small piece of household sponge. Use sponge to dab dark green paint over limbs in random areas.
- Dab on two additional colors of green to create color variation and give tree leaves depth.

- Paint Pine Trees

- Dip tips of a flat paintbrush in paint. Hold brush bristles vertical and lightly dab tips of brush to create a trunk. Dip brush in paint and water as needed.
- Next, hold brush bristles horizontal. Starting at the top of the tree, lightly dab paint with tips of brush to create leaves. (See inset picture for brush stroke.)
- In a triangular pattern, continue dabbing paint until tree is complete.

- Paint Palm Trees

- Paint outline of trunk. Dip brush in paint as needed.
- Dip tips of a flat paintbrush in paint. Holding bristles of brush horizontally, dab and push paintbrush along trunk. Move brush in one direction, either up or down. This will create the unique texture of a palm trunk.
- For leaves, paint a single downward stroke for top of leaf. Then, holding bristle of brush horizontally, make short strokes for bottom of leaf.
- Add additional leaves in a circular pattern. Paint coconuts, if desired.

- Paint Clouds

- Paint sky. Use a dark blue paint for upper portion of sky and light blue paint for lower portion. Blend colors together in middle. (See Blending pg. 159).

- Cut a small piece of household sponge. Dab white paint in a random, cloud-like pattern. Dip sponge in paint as needed. Let dry.

- Dab additional white paint on a few, select areas. This will create color variation and give clouds depth.

- Paint Mountains

To create the illusion of distance, paint the mountain background a light color, the midrange a medium color and the foreground a dark color.

- Paint background mountain in a light color. Brush strokes should be directed up toward centerline of peak.

- Add random colors of browns and greens, as desired. Again, brush strokes should be directed toward center of peak.

- Blend paint together while wet.

- Using the same type of brush strokes, paint a smaller mountain in medium shades.

- Paint another smaller mountain in darker shades.

- Paint darker colors along sides of mountains to add shadows.

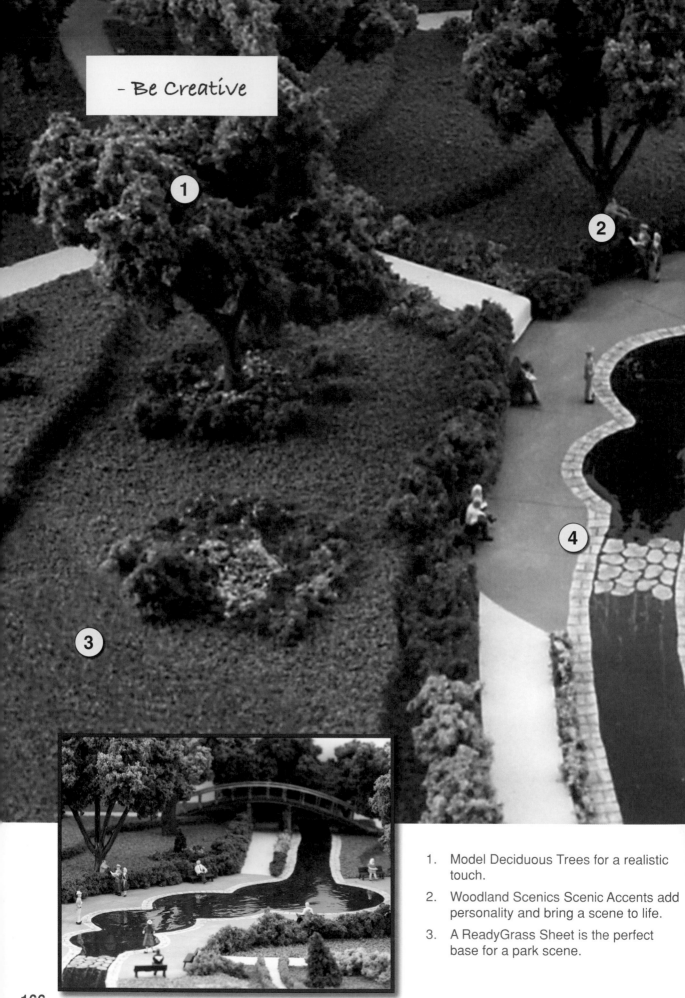

- Be Creative

1. Model Deciduous Trees for a realistic touch.

2. Woodland Scenics Scenic Accents add personality and bring a scene to life.

3. A ReadyGrass Sheet is the perfect base for a park scene.

4. Stone is easily added along the edge of a water feature with an ultra fine point marker and color wash. (See Stone Pattern page 153 and Color Wash page 177)

5. Add a water feature with the Scene-A-Rama Ripplin' Water Kit (SP4122) or Woodland Scenics Water Kit (RG5153).

6. Sprinkle Red or Yellow Flowers on Bushes and Shrubs to model flowers.

7. To clear an area for paths, a water feature or labyrinth, simply dab on water and scrape off turf. (See Remove Turf page 115)

Adhesives & Tools

Project Glue

Project Glue is a thick, strong-hold adhesive that dries clear with a matte finish.

Basic Use

1. Apply Project Glue and press material into adhesive.

    It is great for attaching:

    -   Shrubs and Bushes
    -   Trees
    -   Wild Grass
    -   Rock Castings to a Plaster Cloth terrain

2. **Diluted Project Glue** can be sprayed, brushed or drizzled. (See Project Glue pg. 170)

    -   Seal landscape materials on a diorama.
    -   Create tree foliage.

Sticky Bond

Sticky Bond is an adhesive that dries clear and stays tacky.

Basic Use

1. Brush on Sticky Bond, wait until adhesive is clear and tacky.
2. Press material onto surface of adhesive to adhere.

    It is great for attaching:

    -   Foliage to Tree Armatures
    -   ReadyGrass Sheets

Contact Gluing Method

The contact method provides a fast-setting, permanent bond on non-porous surfaces. It can be done with Project Glue or Sticky Bond.

Basic Use

1. **Contact Method Using Project Glue** is great for assembling a structure, attaching labels to a Backdrop, adding objects to a diorama and more.

   - Apply adhesive on object and surface of contact area.
   - Allow to dry until clear, but no longer than one hour.
   - Press surfaces together.

   NOTE: When brushing on, dip paintbrush in water so glue is easier to spread.

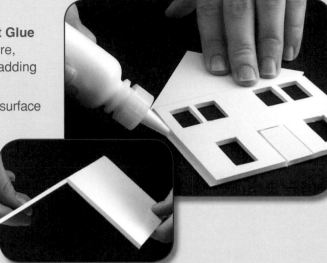

2. **Contact Method Using Sticky Bond** is recommened to attach ReadyGrass Sheets.

   - Apply adhesive on object and surface of contact area.
   - Allow to dry until clear and tacky.
   - Press surfaces together.

Precision Contact Method

This method is useful when placement has to be precise, as with placing a structure or easel in an exact location.

Basic Use

1. Apply a layer of Project Glue on bottom of object and place on desired location.

2. Remove object and set aside until glue becomes clear, but no longer than one hour.

3. Replace object on desired location.

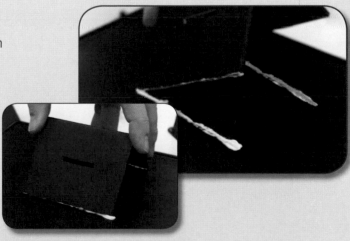

Hobby Knife

A hobby knife is a general purpose cutting tool, commonly used in craft projects. It is popularly known as an X-Acto® knife.

Basic Use

Use a hobby knife under adult supervision. Use with caution.

Make sure your hobby knife is sharp! A dull knife can be dangerous and make a project difficult.

1. A hobby knife must be used with a cutting mat or appropriate cutting surface. Cut with a firm, steady grip.

2. The best way to make a clean, straight-line cut is to use a hobby knife along with a straightedge or ruler. Align the straightedge and run the hobby knife along edge.

Dilutions & Mixtures - mix well

Project Glue

Use diluted Project Glue to attach Green Grass, Accents, Talus, Foliage Fiber and more. Depending on the application, diluted Project Glue is sprayed, brushed or drizzled with an eyedropper.

Project Glue: 1-part Project Glue to 3-parts water

Project Glue in Spray Bottle: Add water to 1/4 mark, then add glue to 1/2 mark - cover Spray Bottle with thumb and shake. Add water to full mark, attach sprayer and shake again.

OPTION: Use a household spray bottle (shake well before inserting spray head). Mix 1-part Project glue with 3-parts water.

Color Wash

Any water-based paint color can be diluted to create a Color Wash. Use a Color Wash to weather structures, highlight textures, age fabrics and more.

Color Wash: 1-part paint to 8-parts water

— Water
— Color

Earth Undercoat

Use diluted Earth Undercoat to paint Plaster Cloth terrain. It provides a natural looking base for landscape materials.

Earth Undercoat: : 1-part Earth Undercoat to 2-parts water

— Water
— Earth Undercoat

Rock Colors

Use Rock Colors to naturally color rock castings. Create Color Washes by diluting Rock Colors in individual cups.

NOTE: The Rock Colors dilution ratio is a guideline. Add more or less water as desired to change color intensity. If diluted Colors are too light, the wide range of shades and intensities will not develop.

Yellow Ocher:
1-part Yellow Ocher to 8-parts water

— Water
— Yellow Ocher

Burnt Umber:
1-part Burnt Umber to 8-parts water

— Water
— Burnt Umber

Black Wash: 1-part Black to 16-parts water

— Water
— Black

Eruption Mixture

Make your volcano erupt with this simple mixture. Use eruption mixture with Scene-A-Rama Volcano Tube, included with Mountain Diorama Kit.

2 oz Vinegar, 1 drop Yellow Food Coloring, 1 drop Red Food Coloring, 2 tsp Baking Soda

1. Add food coloring to vinegar and mix.
2. Pour baking soda into Volcano Tube.
3. Pour vinegar mixture into Tube and watch your volcano erupt.

TIP! For added bubbles, mix 1 drop of liquid dish soap into vinegar mixture.

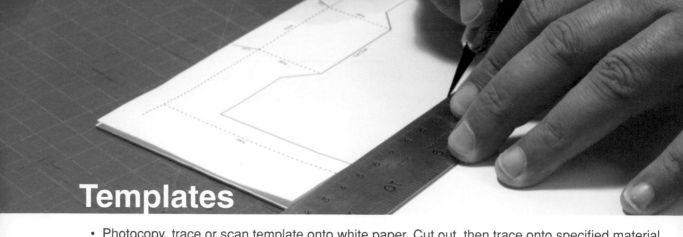

Templates

- Photocopy, trace or scan template onto white paper. Cut out, then trace onto specified material.
- If needed, reduce or enlarge templates to fit your diorama.
- Each template includes basic assembly instructions and needed materials.
- Read through the corresponding project instructions for clarification on using template.
- Short dotted lines -------------- indicate fold lines
- Long dotted lines — — — indicate score lines
- Bold, solid lines ——————— indicate cut lines

Ocean Plants

Aquarium (pg. 10)

- Copy template on white paper or Construction Board (cardstock), then cut out.
- Paint or color, as desired. Attach to diorama with Project Glue.

TIP!
Three-dimensional Look:
Place plants 2 or 3 in a row,
off-setting them slightly.

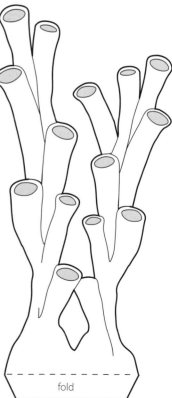

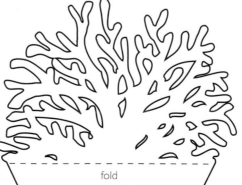

Pyramid

Pyramids of Giza (pg. 60)

- Copy template on white paper, then cut out.

- Trace cutout on Construction Board, then cut out with scissors or hobby knife.

- Score along dotted lines with blunt end of a paintbrush.

- Fold pyramid on score lines. Use a ruler or straightedge for clean folds.

- Cover pyramid with wet Plaster Cloth to add texture.

- Using Project Glue, assemble as shown. Paint, as desired.

Basic Assembly

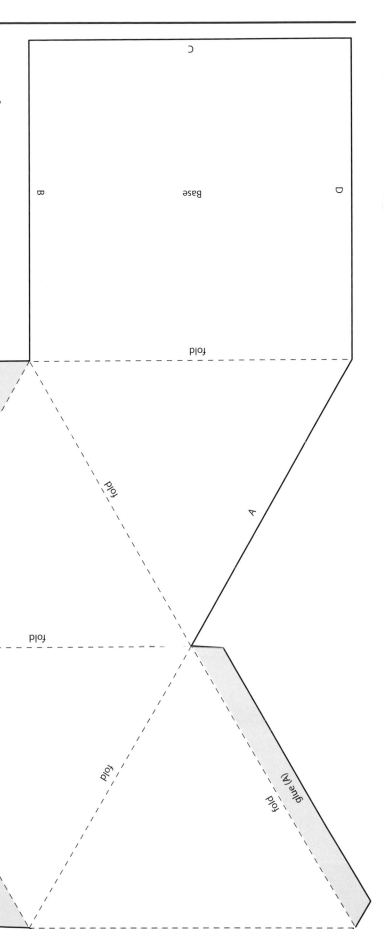

Easel 1

Egyptian Burial Mask (pg. 74), Medusa (pg. 76), Bacteria Cell (pg. 78), Brain Cell (pg. 80), Lungs and Smoking (pg. 85)

- Copy template or trace on white paper.
- Cut out copied template and trace on foam core board, 1/8".
- Cut out with a hobby knife.
- Assemble with Project Glue.
- If using cardstock, make size adjustments.

Tip!
Choose the size stand that best fits your project. (a=smallest, d=largest)

Basic Assembly

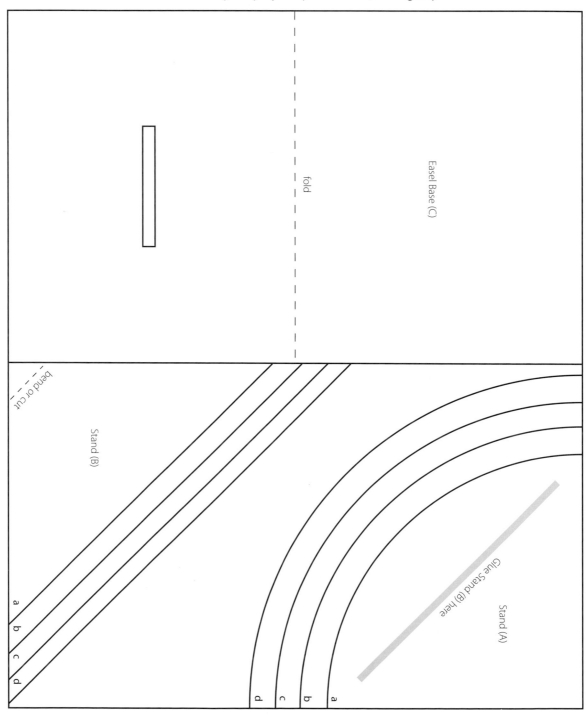

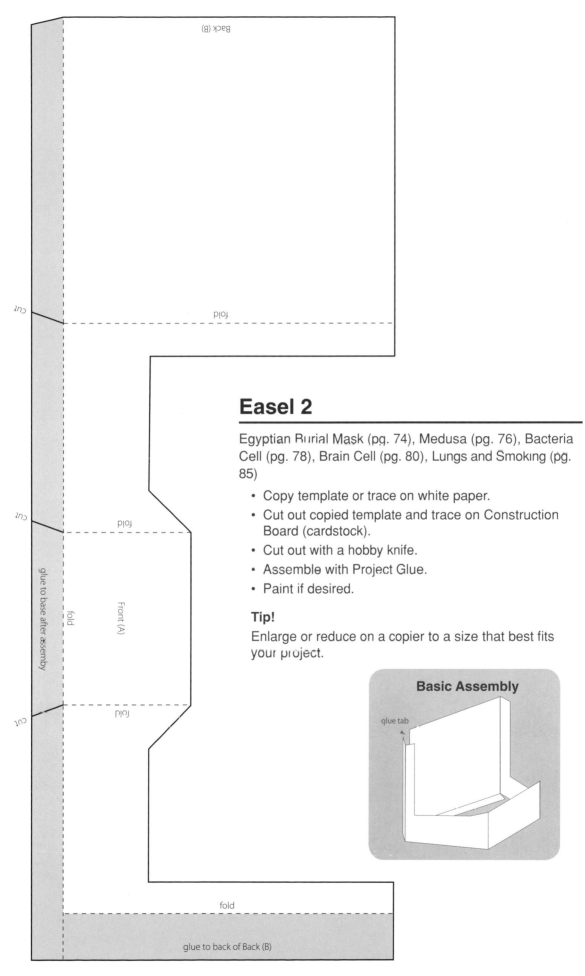

Back (B)

fold

cut

cut

fold

glue to base after assemby

fold

Front (A)

fold

cut

fold

glue to back of Back (B)

Easel 2

Egyptian Burial Mask (pg. 74), Medusa (pg. 76), Bacteria Cell (pg. 78), Brain Cell (pg. 80), Lungs and Smoking (pg. 85)

- Copy template or trace on white paper.
- Cut out copied template and trace on Construction Board (cardstock).
- Cut out with a hobby knife.
- Assemble with Project Glue.
- Paint if desired.

Tip!

Enlarge or reduce on a copier to a size that best fits your project.

Basic Assembly

glue tab

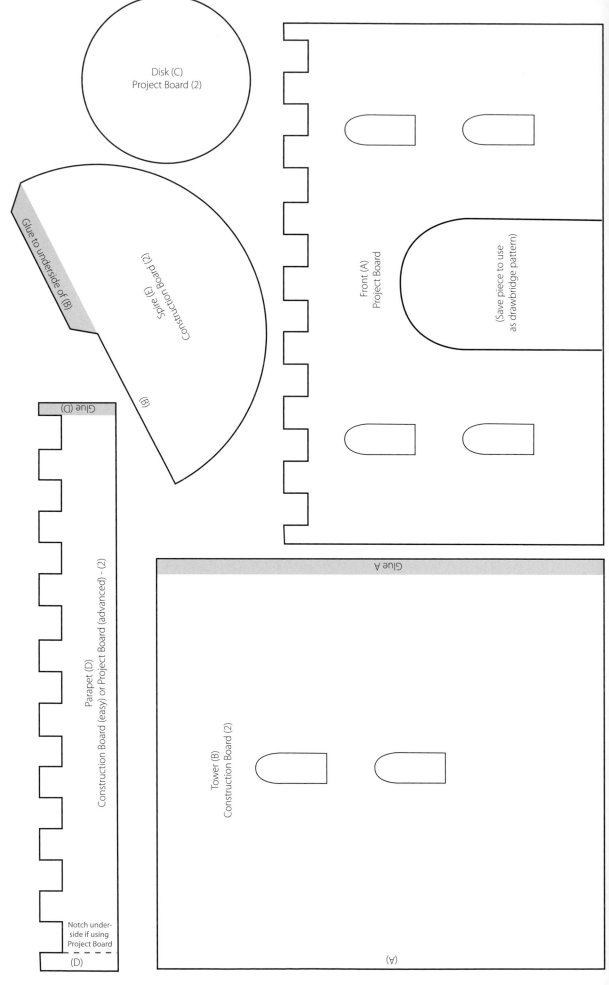

Disk (C)
Project Board (2)

Glue to underside of (B)

Spire (E) (2)
Construction Board (2)

(B)

Front (A)
Project Board

(Save piece to use
as drawbridge pattern)

Glue (D)

Glue A

Parapet (D)
Construction Board (easy) or Project Board (advanced) - (2)

Tower (B)
Construction Board (2)

Notch under-
side if using
Project Board

(D)

(A)

⬅ Medieval Castle

Medieval Castle (pg. 64)

- Copy template on white paper, then cut out.
- Trace cutout on designated material: Project Board or Construction Board.
- Add Brick Pattern (See Buildings and Structures pg. 152)
- Cut out with a hobby knife. Assemble as instructed.

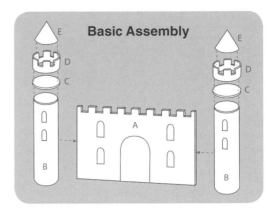

Basic Assembly

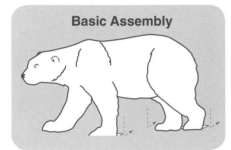

Basic Assembly

Polar Animals

Glaciers and Icebergs (pg. 14)

- Copy template on white paper. Glue to Construction Board (cardstock), then cut out.
- Paint or color, as desired. Attach to diorama with Project Glue.

NOTE: Before attaching, scrape snow mixture from glue points.

Log Cabin

History of Log Cabins (pg. 42)

- Copy template on white paper, then cut out.
- Trace cutouts on listed materials.
- Cut out with a hobby knife.
- Score log pattern (dotted lines) on walls.
- Cut along fold line on underside of roof.
- Assemble with Project Glue.
- Paint, as desired.

TIP!
See Buildings and Structures for assembly and painting ideas.

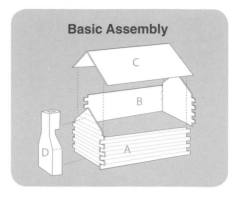

Basic Assembly

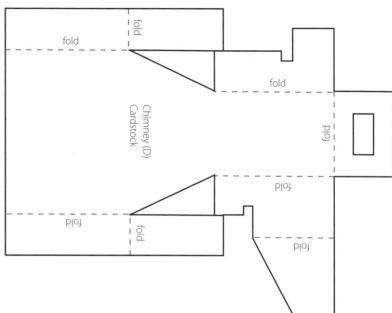

Chimney (D)
Cardstock

fold

Roof (C)
Backdrop Material

score and fold

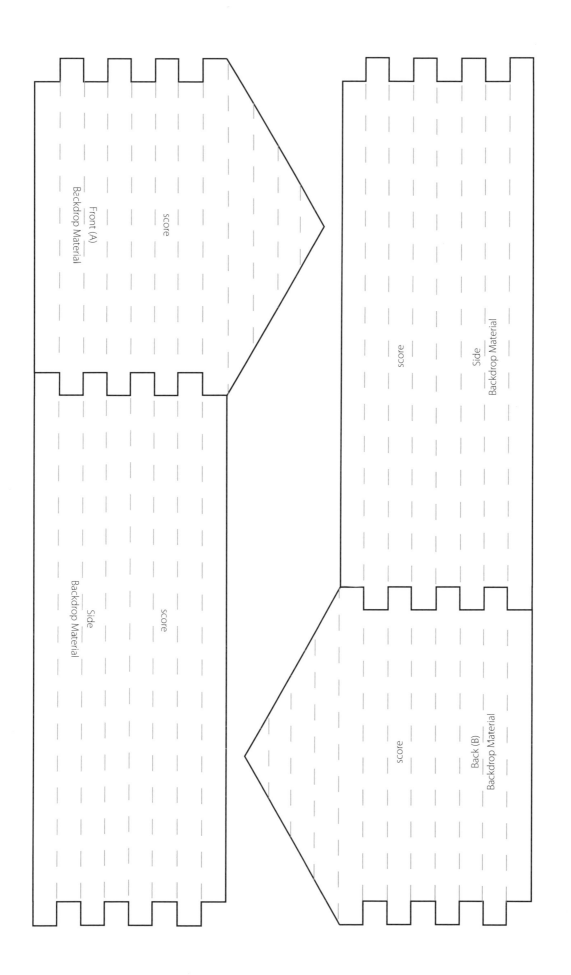

Front (A)
Backdrop Material

score

Side
Backdrop Material

score

Side
Backdrop Material

score

Back (B)
Backdrop Material

score

Egyptian Boat

Life Along the Nile (pg. 55)

- Copy template or trace on white paper, then cut out.
- Trace cutouts onto cardboard with corrugation running horizontally.
- Cut out with scissors (See **TIP!**)
- Assemble as shown using invisible tape or Project Glue. Wrap tape around boat ends for a clean look.

TIP!
Rough cut around all pieces, then flatten with a rolling pin to make cutting with scissors easier. Tape ends in triangle pattern.

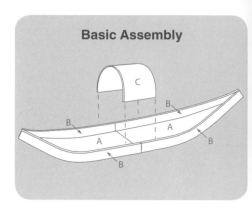

Basic Assembly

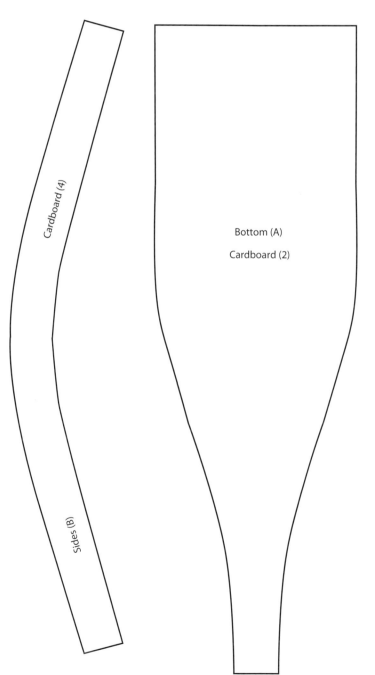

Cardboard (4)

Sides (B)

Bottom (A)

Cardboard (2)

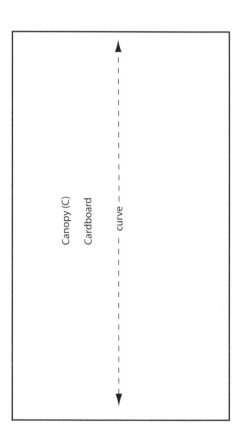

Canopy (C)

Cardboard

curve

Egyptian Sphinx, Pyramid and Walkway

Life Along the Nile (pg. 55)

- Copy template on white paper, then cut out.
- Trace cutouts onto Project Board.
- Cut out with a hobby knife and assemble with Project Glue.

Basic Assembly

glue in place

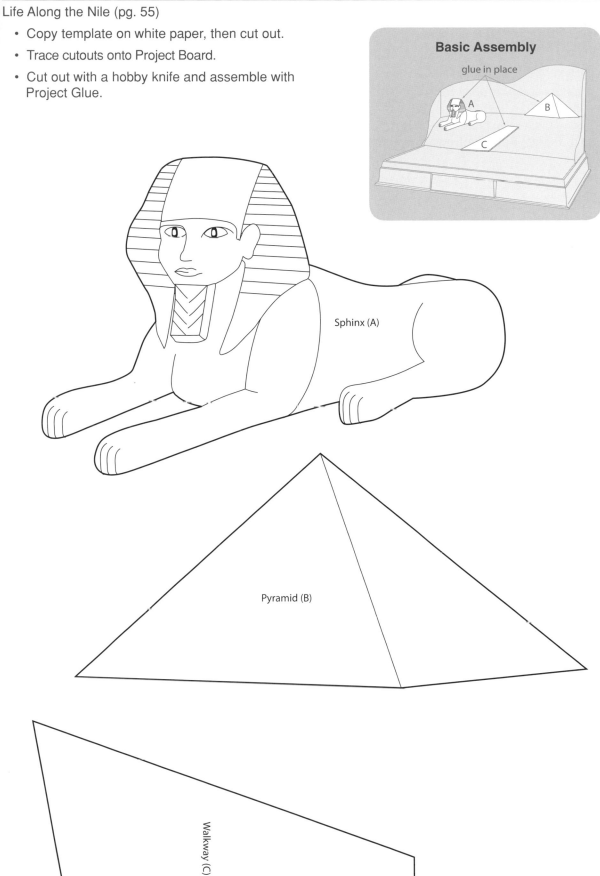

Sphinx (A)

Pyramid (B)

Walkway (C)

Cliff Dwelling

Cliff Dwellings (pg. 36)

- Copy template on white paper, then cut out.
- Trace cutout on Sculpting Clay or Construction Board.
- Assemble with Project Glue.
- Attach beams (Project Sticks or twigs found outside) in notches.
- Using ladder template as a guide, assemble ladder with Project Sticks or twigs found outside.

TIP!
Save window cut-outs for window and door coverings.

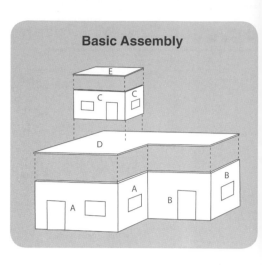

Basic Assembly

Second Story Placement

Ladder Opening

First Story Roof (D)

Second Story Roof (E)

Ladder Opening

First Story Ladder

Second Story Ladder

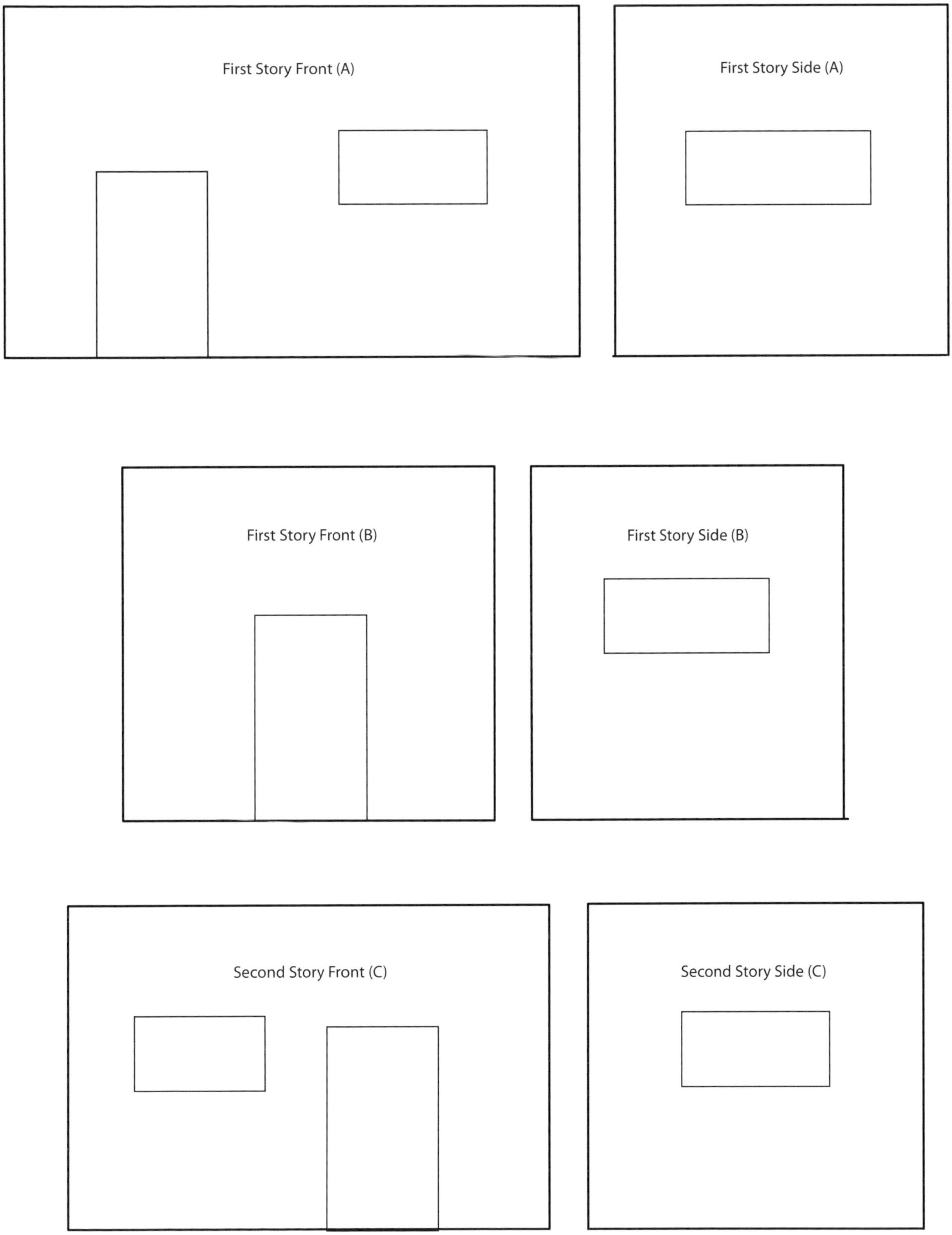

First Story Front (A)

First Story Side (A)

First Story Front (B)

First Story Side (B)

Second Story Front (C)

Second Story Side (C)

Native American Tepee

Tepee Life (pg. 40)

- Copy template on white paper, then cut out.
- Glue cutout on Project Cloth. Cut out and assemble as shown. Paint, as desired.

Native American Canoe

Tepee Life (pg. 40)

- Copy template on white paper, then cut out.
- Trace cutout on Construction Board, then cut out.
- Using Project Glue, assemble as shown.
- Paint, as desired.

TIP!

Use small stick inside Canoe to hold shape while drying.

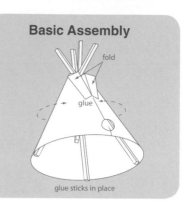

Basic Assembly

fold

glue

glue sticks in place

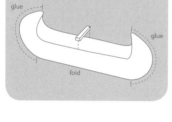

Basic Assembly

glue

glue

fold

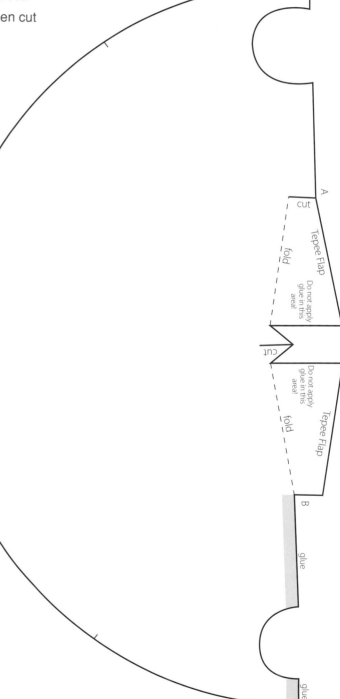

A

cut

Tepee Flap

fold

Do not apply glue in this area!

cut

Do not apply glue in this area!

Tepee Flap

fold

B

glue

glue

Tepee Lodge Pole Guide

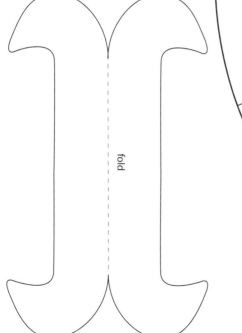

fold

The Alamo

The Alamo (pg. 50)

- Copy template on white paper, then cut out.
- Trace cutout on listed materials.
- Cut out using a hobby knife.
- Using Project Glue, assemble as shown.

Basic Assembly

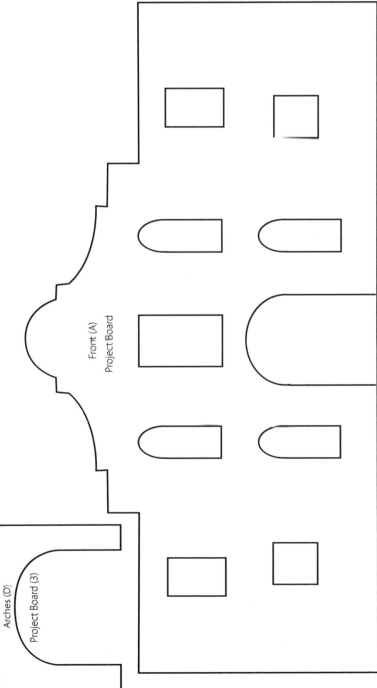

Front (A)
Project Board

Arches (D)
Project Board (3)

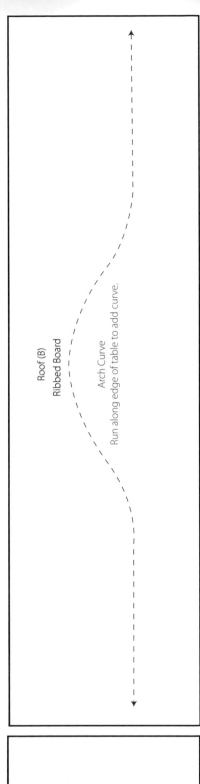

Roof (B)
Ribbed Board

Arch Curve
Run along edge of table to add curve.

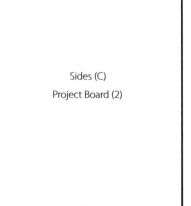

Sides (C)
Project Board (2)

Exploration Ship

Exploration (pg. 46)

- Copy the template on white paper, then cut out.
- Trace cutouts on listed materials.
- Cut pieces out with hobby knife.
- Assemble as shown using Project Glue.
- See Exploration (pg. 46) for details.

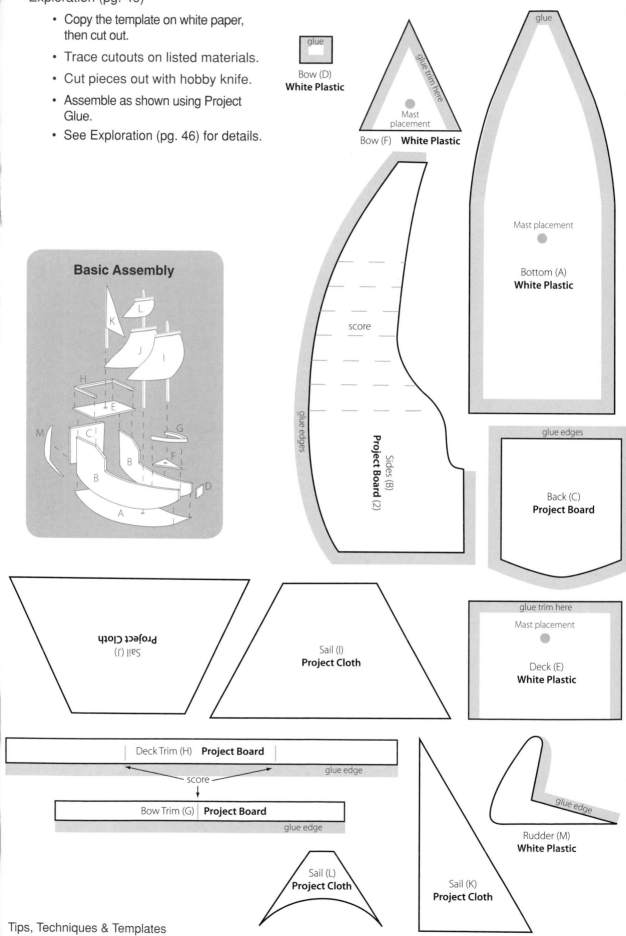

glue

Bow (D)
White Plastic

glue trim here

Mast placement

Bow (F) **White Plastic**

glue

Mast placement

Bottom (A)
White Plastic

Basic Assembly

L

K

J

I

H

E

M

C

G

B

F

B

D

A

score

glue edges

Sides (B)
Project Board (2)

glue edges

Back (C)
Project Board

glue trim here

Mast placement

Deck (E)
White Plastic

Sail (J)
Project Cloth

Sail (I)
Project Cloth

Deck Trim (H) **Project Board**

glue edge

score

Bow Trim (G) **Project Board**

glue edge

glue edge

Rudder (M)
White Plastic

Sail (L)
Project Cloth

Sail (K)
Project Cloth

Covered Wagon

Exploration (pg. 46), Santa Fe Trail
Pioneers (pg. 48)

- Copy the template on white paper,
  then cut out.
- Trace cutouts on listed materials.
- Cut out pieces with hobby knife.
- Assemble as instructed using Project
  Glue (pg. 47).

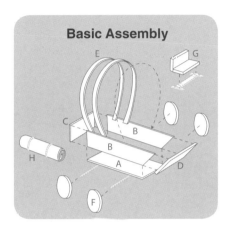

Basic Assembly

Bottom (A)
White Plastic

Cover (H)
(Roll up or cover wagon)
Project Cloth

Hoops (E) **White Plastic** (4˝

Wheels (F)
Project Board (4)

Sides (B)
Project Board

Front (D)
Project Board

score and fold
Seat (G)
Project Board

Back (C)
Project Board

Lungs

Lungs and Smoking (pg. 85)

- Use a copier to shrink or enlarge the lung templates. Enlarge Lungs Template by 25% when using the Large Project Base & Backdrop.

- Cut out copied template, trace cutout on cardboard, then cut out.

- See step-by-step instructions for assembly informaton.

Basic Assembly

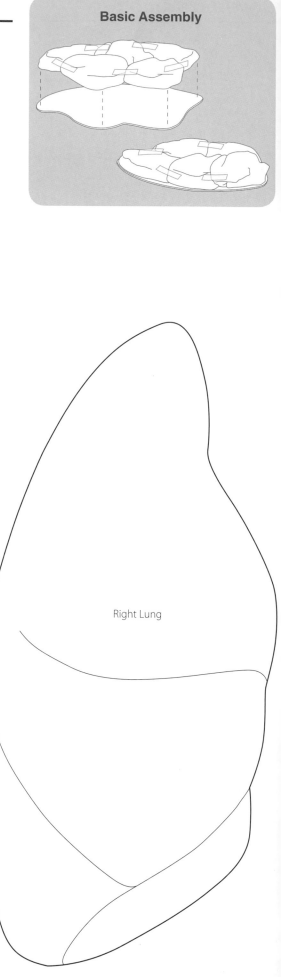

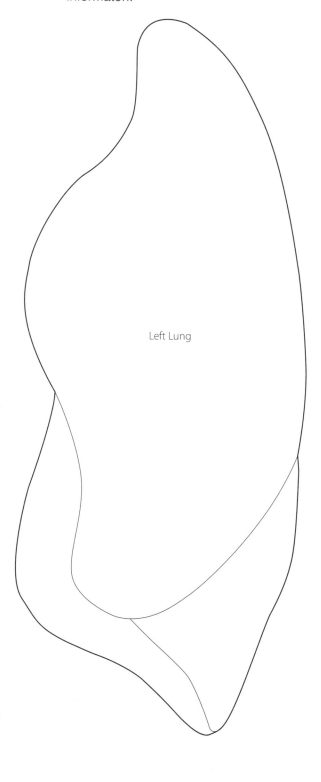

Left Lung

Right Lung

Scene-A-Rama is a product line full of easy-to-use, realistic materials designed to create one-of-a-kind school projects, dioramas, displays, arts and crafts.

Project Base & Backdrop

Project Bases come in two sizes: large and small. The included Backdrops are great for backgrounds, horizons or labeling project parts. Also includes labels and double-stick tape for easy assembly.

Project Base & Backdrop Large SP4165
Overall Size: 18"w x 12 $^1\!/_2$"d x 13 $^1\!/_8$"h
Project Area: 16 $^1\!/_4$"w x 10 $^3\!/_4$"d x 11"h

Project Base & Backdrop Small SP4166
Overall Size: 12 $^1\!/_2$"w x 9 $^1\!/_4$"d x 9 $^5\!/_8$"h
Project Area: 10 $^3\!/_4$"w x 7 $^3\!/_8$"d x 7 $^1\!/_2$"h

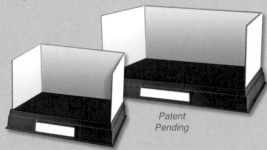

Patent Pending

ShowBox™ SP4167

The ShowBox is great for shoebox dioramas. It is constructed of sturdy, white material. Paint, decorate, label or use the box as is. Labels included.

Overall Size: 13 $^1\!/_2$"w x 4 $^1\!/_2$"d x 10"h

Inside Dimensions: 13"w x 4 $^1\!/_2$"d x 8 $^1\!/_2$"h

Trees

Add realistic, ready-to-use trees and watch your diorama or display come to life!

Deciduous	Conifer	Palm	Autumn
SP4150	SP4151	SP4152	SP4153

ReadyGrass® Sheets

Attach to Project Base to represent grass or sand. Available in three colors.

Sheet size: 10 $^3\!/_4$" x 16 $^1\!/_4$"

Summer Grass	Green Grass	Desert Sand
SP4160	SP4161	SP4162

Building & Structure Kit SP4130

Create buildings, structures, geometric shapes and more.

Kit Contents
- Project Boards
- Project Cloth
- Project Sticks
- Clear Plastic
- Construction Board
- White Plastic
- Black Paper
- Ribbed Board
- Project Wire
- Project Glue
- Easy Instructions

Sculpting Kit SP4131

Make figures, animals and shapes for your projects. Includes paints, tools, tips and techniques.

Kit Contents
- Sculpting Clay
- Sculpting Tool
- Project Paints
- Paintbrush
- Fun Fur
- Project Wire
- Project Glue
- Easy Instructions

Horizon and Detail Kit SP4132

Make horizons and backgrounds. Includes cloud and mountain-making materials.

Kit Contents
- Plaster Cloth
- Project Paints
- Foliage Fiber
- Green Grass
- Puffy Clouds
- Project Wire
- Paintbrush ($^1\!/_2$")
- Paintbrush ($^1\!/_8$")
- Project Glue
- Easy Instructions

Plaster Cloth and Casting Plaster

Plaster Cloth SP4140
Use Plaster Cloth to make masks, hard land surfaces, ornaments and more. Forms over almost any shape!

Plaster Cloth SP4141
Use Casting Plaster to cast rocks, fossils, tracks and more. Use for any mold or impression.

Diorama Kits

The four Diorama Kits include the materials needed to make a realistic environment for your project. Built on a Project Base & Backdrop or other flat surface. Choose from a basic landscape, a mountain or volcano, water or desert oasis.

Basic Diorama Kit SP4110

This kit includes a ReadyGrass Sheet for an instant, grassy flat area.

Kit Contents
- Green Grass ReadyGrass
- 6-Tree Armatures
- Foliage Fiber
- Shrubs
- Wild Grass
- Yellow Flowers
- Evergreen Accent
- Forest Green Accent
- Sticky Bond
- Project Glue
- Spray Bottle
- Foam Brush
- Plastic Cup and Sifter Lid
- Stir Stick
- Easy Instructions

Mountain Diorama Kit SP4111

Make mountains, volcanoes, hills, caves, erosion or land contours with rock outcroppings.Use earth-colored paint, grasses, bushes, soils, vines and rock debris to create scenery.

Kit Contents
- Earth Undercoat
- Rock Colors
- Volcano Tube
- Shrubs
- Foliage Fiber
- Green Grass
- Evergreen Accent
- Forest Green Accent
- Rock Mold
- Casting Plaster
- Talus
- Side Panels
- Plaster Cloth
- Project Glue
- Spray Bottle
- Mixing Tray
- Foam Brush
- Plastic Cup and Sifter Lid
- Stir Stick
- Easy Instructions

Desert Oasis Diorama Kit SP4112

Model shorelines, wastelands or other desert scenery. Use as settings for missions, prehistoric habitats or other sandy settings.

Kit Contents
- Desert Sand ReadyGrass
- 5-Palm Trees (4"- 5")
- Foliage Fiber
- Wild Grass
- Green Grass
- Yellow Flowers
- Talus
- Sticky Bond
- Project Glue
- Spray Bottle
- Foam Brush
- Plastic Cup and Sifter Lid
- Stir Stick
- Easy Instructions

Water Diorama Kit SP4113

Model still or moving water features, such as lakes, rivers and waterfalls. Landscape your scene with earth-colored pigment, short and tall grasses, bushes and vines.

Kit Contents
- Realistic Water
- Water Effects
- Water Undercoat
- Earth Undercoat
- Side Panels
- Plaster Cloth
- Shrubs
- Foliage Fiber
- Green Grass
- Evergreen Accent
- Forest Green Accent
- Talus
- Project Glue
- Spray Bottle
- Foam Brush
- Plastic Cup and Sifter Lid
- Stir Stick
- Release Paper
- Easy Instructions

Accent Kits

Add foliage and grasses, rocks, water, desert plants and winter effects. They give your project that added detail.

Foliage & Grasses SP4120

Add bushes, shrubs, flowers, weeds and grasses to a diorama.

Kit Contents
- Foliage Fiber
- Bushes
- Green Grass
- Forest Green Accent
- Yellow Flowers
- Project Glue
- Wild Grass
- Spray Bottle
- Sifter
- Easy Instructions

Rock Making Kit SP4121

Use a Rock Mold to create a multitude of rock formations with Casting Plaster.

Kit Contents
- Rock Mold
- Casting Plaster
- Rock Colors
- Talus
- Mixing Tray
- Foam Brush
- Stir Stick
- Project Glue
- Easy Instructions

Ripplin' Water Kit SP4122

Create lakes, rivers, waterfalls, rapids, waves and more.

Kit Contents
- Realistic Water
- Water Effects
- Water Undercoat
- Foam Brush
- Stir Stick
- Release Paper
- Easy Instructions

Winter Effects SP4123

Enhance your project with realistic cold-weather icy and snowy details.

Kit Contents
- Ice Effects
- Snowflakes
- Snow Base
- Foam Brush
- Plastic Cup & Sifter Lid
- Stir Stick
- Release Paper
- Easy Instructions

Desert Plants SP4124

Includes a variety of cacti, flowers, grasses and brush.

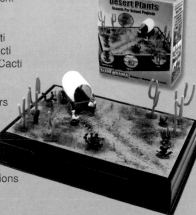

Kit Contents
- Saguaro Cacti
- Columnar Cacti
- Prickly Pear Cacti
- Barrel Cacti
- Red Flowers
- Yellow Flowers
- Wild Grass
- Foliage Fiber
- Project Glue
- Easy Instructions

Scene Setters™

Bring your school projects and dioramas to life! Scene Setters are collections of themed sets of people, animals and a variety of specialized items sized just right for dioramas, displays and other projects. You will find fun, educational information included on the packaging of each set of Scene Setters.

Egyptian Culture
SP4341

Castle Dwellers
SP4342

Native Americans
SP4343

Native American Hunt
SP4344

American Civil War
SP4345

Marine Life
SP4347

African Wildlife
SP4346

North American Wildlife
SP4349

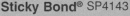
Prehistoric Life
SP4350

Alternative Energy
SP4348

Adhesives

Project Glue™ SP4142
Project Glue is a multipurpose, water-soluble adhesive. Safe for kids.

Sticky Bond® SP4143
Sticky Bond is great for bonding ReadyGrass Sheets to Project Bases and attaching foliage to Tree Armatures. Stays tacky.

SCENE-A-RAMA® *Photo Glossary*

This photo glossary briefly describes our Scene-A-Rama products, their intended use and the kit(s) that include these materials. Where the glossary indicates 'replace with Woodland Scenics,' we've included the Woodland Scenics product name and item number necessary to purchase the product separately. Scene-A-Rama is a division of Woodland Scenics®, a company that specializes in model scenery products used for model railroads, architectural models, wargaming layouts, collectible house displays and other hobbies. For more information about these and other products, visit woodlandscenics.com. *All Scene-A-Rama and Woodland Scenics products are ASTM certified.*

◇ Caution   ♥ Modeling and Care Information

Accents

Foliage product to add texture and highlights to grasses, trees, bushes, vines and more.

Colors: Evergreen, Forest Green

Included with: Basic Diorama Kit, Foliage & Grasses, Mountain Diorama Kit, Water Diorama Kit

Replace with Woodland Scenics: Dark Green Coarse Turf (T65), Weeds Fine Turf (T46)

Black Paper

Black construction paper. Use to add depth to a building, model a road, blacken windows and more.

Included with: Building & Structure Kit

Bushes

Foliage product to model bushes, shrubs and trees.

Color: Dark Green

Included with: Foliage & Grasses

Replace with Woodland Scenics: Dark Green Bushes (FC147)

Casting Plaster

Lightweight plaster to cast rocks, make impressions, create lava flow and more.

Included with: Mountain Diorama Kit, Rock Making Kit

◇ Do not take internally. Keep out of reach of children. Do not make body casts. If Casting Plaster is allowed to harden in contact with skin, it can develop heat sufficient to cause burns.

♥ Wash with warm, soapy water. If plaster dries on clothes or project area, rub off with a soft brush before washing.

Clear Plastic

Sheet of clear .005 Styrene for modeling windows.

Included with: Building & Structure Kit

Construction Board

High quality cardstock. Use to model buildings, pyramids, project details and more.

Included with: Building & Structure Kit

Desert Plants

Four types of cacti to model a desert scene.

Included with: Desert Plants

Earth Undercoat

Liquid earth-colored pigment to color Plaster Cloth terrain.

Included with: Mountain Diorama Kit, Water Diorama Kit

Replace with Woodland Scenics: Earth Colors™ Liquid Pigment Earth Undercoat (C1229)

♥ Clean spills immediately with warm, soapy water.

Flowers

Model flowers on bushes, shrubs, vines, fields and trees.

Colors: Red, Yellow

Included with: Basic Diorama Kit, Desert Oasis Diorama Kit, Desert Plants, Foliage & Grasses

Replace with Woodland Scenics: Flowers (T48)

Foam Brush

Craft paintbrush with a 3/4" foam head.

Included with: most Scene-A-Rama kits

Foliage Fiber

Green fiber to model vines, undergrowth, trees and more.

Included with: Basic Diorama Kit, Desert Oasis Diorama Kit, Desert Plants, Foliage & Grasses, Horizon & Detail Kit, Mountain Diorama Kit, Water Diorama Kit

Replace with Woodland Scenics: Poly Fiber (FP178)

Fun Fur

Fiber to model animal fur, hair and facial hair.

Included with: Sculpting Kit

Green Grass

Foliage product to model grass.

Color: Green

Included with: Foliage & Grasses, Horizon & Detail Kit, Desert Oasis Diorama Kit, Water Diorama Kit,

Replace with Woodland Scenics: Green Grass Fine Turf (T45)

Ice Effects

Product to model frozen ponds, icy areas and more.

Included with: Winter Effects

Replace with Woodland Scenics: Realistic Water™ (C1211)

♥ Wash with warm, soapy water. Should plaster dry on clothes or project area, rub off with a soft brush before washing.

Mixing Tray

Tray to mix Rock Colors and Casting Plaster.

Included with: Rock Making Kit, Mountain Diorama Kit

Paintbrushes

Available in two sizes: 1/8" and 1/2".

Included with: Horizon & Detail Kit, Sculpting Kit

Plaster Cloth

Cloth infused with plaster on the surface. Use to create a hard shell.

Included with: Mountain Diorama Kit, Water Diorama Kit, Horizon & Detail Kit

◇ Do not take internally. Keep out of reach of children. Do not make body casts. If Plaster Cloth is allowed to harden in contact with skin, it can develop heat sufficient to cause burns.

♥ Wash with warm, soapy water. Should plaster dry on clothes or project area, rub off with a soft brush before washing.

Plastic Cup

Plastic cup for diluted mixtures.

Included with: Basic Diorama Kit, Desert Oasis Diorama Kit, Foliage & Grasses, Mountain Diorama Kit, Water Diorama Kit, Winter Effects

Plastic Cup & Sifter Lid

Plastic cup and hole-punched lid used for applying Accents.

Included with: Basic Diorama Kit, Desert Oasis Diorama Kit, Foliage & Grasses, Mountain Diorama Kit, Water Diorama Kit, Winter Effects

Project Board

Durable piece of foam core board. Use to model buildings, create a castle, add texture to structures and more

Included with: Building & Structure Kit

Project Cloth

Versatile cream-colored cloth. Use to model a tepee, cover a stagecoach, make curtains and more.

Included with: Building & Structure Kit

Project Glue

White craft glue that dries clear with a matte finish.

Included with: most Scene-A-Rama kits

♥ Clean spills immediately with warm, soapy water.

Project Paints

Concentrated craft paints.

Included with: Horizon & Detail Kit, Sculpting Kit

♥ Clean spills immediately with warm, soapy water.

Project Sticks

Square wooden sticks, 10" x 1/16". Use to model a tepee, drawbridge, fire pit and more.

Included with: Building & Structure Kit

Project Wire

Bendable craft wire (.026).

Included with: Building & Structure Kit, Sculpting Kit, Horizon & Detail Kit

ReadyGrass Sheets

Non-shedding, vinyl grass mat.

Colors: Desert Sand, Green Grass, Summer Grass

Included with: Basic Diorama Kit, Desert Oasis Diorama Kit

Realistic Water

Product used to model water areas.

Included with: Ripplin' Water Kit, Water Diorama Kit

Replace with Woodland Scenics: Realistic Water (C1211)

♥ Clean spills immediately with warm, soapy water.

Release Paper

Freezer paper used with Water Effects.

Included with: Ripplin' Water Kit, Water Diorama Kit, Winter Effects

Ribbed Board

Single-faced corrugated cardboard. Use to create buildings, Spanish tile roof, corrugated metal and more.

Included with: Building & Structure Kit

Rock Colors

Liquid pigments designed to color rocks with realistic results.

Included with: Mountain Diorama Kit, Rock Making Kit

Replace with Woodland Scenics: Earth Colors Liquid Pigment (C1220, C1222, C1223)

Rock Mold

Used with Casting Plaster to cast realistic rocks.

Included with: Mountain Diorama Kit, Rock Making Kit

Sculpting Clay

Air-dry modeling clay. Use to sculpt, add texture to a Plaster Cloth project and more.

Included with: Sculpting Kit

Sculpting Tool

Tool used with sculpting clay.

Included with: Sculpting Kit

Shrubs

Dense foliage product to model shrubs, bushes, trees and more.

Colors: Medium Green

Included with: Basic Diorama Kit, Mountain Diorama Kit, Water Diorama Kit

Replace with Woodland Scenics: Medium Green Clump-Foliage (FC683)

Side Panels

Cardboard panels used to create terrain features.

Included with: Mountain Diorama Kit, Water Diorama Kit

Snow Base

A White latex paint used as a basecoat with Snowflakes.

Included with: Winter Effects

♥ Clean spills immediately with warm, soapy water.

Snowflakes

Use to model a realistic snow fall.

Included with: Winter Effects

Replace with Woodland Scenics: Soft Flake Snow™ (SN140)

Spray Bottle

Spray bottle used to apply diluted Project Glue.

Included with: Basic Diorama Kit, Desert Oasis Diorama Kit, Foliage & Grasses, Mountain Diorama Kit, Water Diorama Kit

Sticky Bond

Contact adhesive to attach ReadyGrass Sheets and Foliage to Tree Armatures.

Included with: Basic Diorama Kit, Desert Oasis Diorama Kit

♥ Clean spills immediately with warm, soapy water.

Stir Stick

Disposable craft stick.

Included with: most Scene-A-Rama kits

Talus

Lightweight material designed to model rock debris.

Colors: Natural, Brown

Included with: Desert Oasis Diorama Kit, Mountain Diorama Kit, Rock Making Kit, Water Diorama Kit

Replace with Woodland Scenics: Fine Natural (C1282), Medium Natural (C1283), Fine Brown (C1274), Medium Brown (C1275)

Tree Armatures

Bendable, plastic tree forms to model trees.

Style and Size: Deciduous 2" – 5"

Included with: Basic Diorama Kit

Replace with Woodland Scenics: 2"-3" Tree Armatures (TR1121), 3"-5" Tree Armatures (TR1122)

Volcano Tube

Clear plastic cylinder. Holds Eruption Mixture when creating a volcano.

Included with: Mountain Diorama Kit

Water Effects

White paste that dries clear. Used to create interest and texture in water features.

Included with: Ripplin' Water Kit, Water Diorama Kit

Replace with Woodland Scenics: Water Effects (C1212)

♥ Clean spills immediately with warm, soapy water.

Water Undercoat

Slate blue latex paint used as a base color for water areas.

Included with: Ripplin' Water Kit, Water Diorama Kit

♥ Clean spills immediately with warm, soapy water.

White Fiber

White fiber used to create clouds, volcano smoke and more.

Included with: Horizon & Detail Kit

White Plastic

Sheet of .020 styrene used to add details to buildings.

Included with: Building & Structure Kit

Wild Grass

Model tall and short grasses, weeds and more.

Colors: Harvest Gold, Medium Green

Included with: Basic Diorama Kit, Desert Oasis Diorama Kit, Desert Plants, Foliage & Grasses

Replace with Woodland Scenics: Harvest Gold Field Grass (FG172), Medium Green Field Grass (FG174)

Enhance your diorama with other Woodland Scenics products!

Scenic Accents®

Figures, animals and accessories to add interest and life to a diorama or display.

AutoScenes®

More than just a car, it is a clever scene to add personality to a diorama or display.

Flex Paste™

An extremely versatile product used to smooth rough surfaces, seal water areas on Plaster Cloth terrain, add a stucco finish to buildings and much more.

Woodland Scenics Trees

Complete line of trees, from conifer to deciduous to enhance a diorama or display.

When making a project following the step-by-step instructions, you may not use all the materials included in the Scene-A-Rama kit(s). Here is a list of what you will use. Remember, there is no wrong way to build a diorama. Feel free to use more or less of the kit contents as you desire.

Aquarium (pg. 10-11)
Sculpting Kit
- Sculpting Clay
- Project Paints
- Project Glue
- Project Wire
- Sculpting Tool
- Paintbrush

Coastal Tide Pool (pg. 12-13)
Water Diorama Kit
- Side Panels
- Plaster Cloth
- Plastic Cup & Sifter Lid
- Project Glue
- Spray Bottle
- Realistic Water
- Earth Undercoat
- Stir Stick
- Foam Brush
- Green Grass
- Evergreen Accent
- Forest Green Accent
- Shrubs
- Talus
- Foliage Fiber

Sculpting Kit
- Sculpting Clay
- Project Paints
- Project Glue
- Sculpting Tool
- Paintbrush

Glaciers & Icebergs
(pg. 14-15)
Winter Effects
- Snow Base
- Snowflakes
- Plastic Cup & Sifter Lid
- Foam Brush
- Stir Stick

Ripplin' Water Kit
- Water Undercoat
- Foam Brush
- Realistic Water
- Water Effects

Icebergs (pg. 16-17)
Winter effects
- Foam Brush
- Stir Stick
- Snow Base
- Snowflakes
- Plastic Cup & Sifter Lid

Ripplin' Water Kit
- Water Undercoat
- Foam Brush
- Stir Stick
- Realistic Water
- Water Effects

Igloo Life (pg. 18-19)
Winter Effects
- Snowflakes
- Snow Base
- Plastic Cup & Sifter Lid
- Stir Stick
- Foam Brush

Amazon Basin (pg. 20-22)
Water Diorama Kit
- Side Panels
- Plaster Cloth
- Plastic Cup & Sifter Lid
- Project Glue
- Spray Bottle
- Realistic Water
- Earth Undercoat
- Water Effects
- Stir Stick
- Foam Brush
- Release Paper
- Green Grass
- Evergreen Accent
- Forest Green Accent
- Shrubs
- Talus
- Foliage Fiber

**Environmental
Effects** (pg. 23-25)
Water Diorama Kit
- Side Panels
- Plaster Cloth
- Plastic Cup & Sifter Lid
- Project Glue
- Spray Bottle
- Realistic Water
- Earth Undercoat
- Stir Stick
- Foam Brush
- Green Grass
- Evergreen Accent
- Forest Green Accent
- Shrubs
- Talus
- Foliage Fiber

African Wildlife (pg. 26-27)
Water Diorama Kit
- Side Panels
- Plaster Cloth
- Plastic Cup & Sifter Lid
- Project Glue
- Spray Bottle
- Realistic Water
- Earth Undercoat
- Water Undercoat
- Stir Stick
- Foam Brush
- Green Grass
- Evergreen Accent
- Forest Green Accent
- Shrubs
- Talus
- Foliage Fiber

North American Wildlife
(pg. 28-30)
Mountain Diorama Kit
- Side Panels
- Plaster Cloth
- Casting Plaster
- Rock Mold, Mixing Tray
- Rock Colors
- Earth Undercoat
- Talus
- Foliage Fiber
- Green Grass
- Evergreen Accent
- Forest Green Accent,
- Shrubs
- Plastic Cup & Sifter Lid
- Spray Bottle
- Foam Brush
- Stir Stick
- Project Glue

Winter Effects
- All kit contents used.

Prehistoric Life (pg. 31-33)
Mountain Diorama Kit
- Side Panels
- Plaster Cloth
- Casting Plaster
- Rock Mold, Mixing Tray
- Rock Colors
- Earth Undercoat
- Talus
- Foliage Fiber
- Green Grass
- Evergreen Accent
- Forest Green Accent
- Shrubs
- Plastic Cup & Sifter Lid
- Spray Bottle
- Foam Brush
- Stir Stick
- Project Glue

Native American Hunt
(pg. 34-35)
Mountain Diorama Kit
- Side Panels
- Plaster Cloth
- Casting Plaster
- Rock Mold, Mixing Tray
- Rock Colors
- Earth Undercoat
- Talus
- Foliage Fiber
- Green Grass
- Evergreen Accent
- Forest Green Accent
- Shrubs
- Plastic Cup & Sifter Lid
- Spray Bottle
- Foam Brush
- Stir Stick
- Project Glue

Cliff Dwellings (pg. 36-39)
Mountain Diorama Kit
- Side Panels
- Plaster Cloth
- Casting Plaster
- Rock Mold
- Mixing Tray
- Rock Colors
- Earth Undercoat
- Talus
- Foliage Fiber
- Green Grass
- Evergreen Accent
- Forest Green Accent
- Shrubs
- Plastic Cup & Sifter Lid
- Spray Bottle
- Foam Brush
- Stir Stick
- Project Glue

Sculpting Kit
- Sculpting Clay
- Project Paints
- Project Glue
- Sculpting Tool
- Paintbrush

Tepee Life (pg. 40-41)
Building & Structure Kit
- Project Cloth
- Clear Plastic
- Project Sticks
- Construction Board
- Project Wire
- Project Glue

Horizon & Detail Kit
- Plaster Cloth
- Project Paints
- Project Glue
- Paintbrushes
- Green Grass
- Foliage Fiber
- White Fiber

History of Log Cabins
(pg. 42-43)
Mountain Diorama Kit
- Side Panels
- Plaster Cloth
- Casting Plaster
- Rock Mold
- Mixing Tray
- Rock Colors
- Earth Undercoat
- Talus
- Foliage Fiber
- Green Grass
- Evergreen Accent
- Forest Green Accent
- Shrubs
- Plastic Cup & Sifter Lid
- Spray Bottle
- Foam Brush
- Stir Stick
- Project Glue

Ripplin' Water Kit
- Water Undercoat
- Realistic Water
- Stir Stick
- Foam Brush

Civil War Battle of Wilson's Creek (pg. 44-45)
Mountain Diorama Kit
- Side Panels
- Plaster Cloth
- Casting Plaster
- Rock Mold
- Mixing Tray
- Rock Colors
- Earth Undercoat
- Talus
- Foliage Fiber
- Green Grass
- Evergreen Accent
- Forest Green Accent
- Shrubs
- Plastic Cup & Sifter Lid
- Spray Bottle
- Foam Brush
- Stir Stick
- Project Glue

Ripplin' Water Kit
- Water Undercoat
- Realistic Water
- Stir Stick
- Foam Brush

Exploration (pg. 46-47)
Building & Structure Kit
- Project Cloth
- Project Board
- White Plastic
- Construction Board
- Project Stick
- Project Glue

Santa Fe Trail Pioneers (pg. 48-49)
Desert Plants
- All kit contents used.

The Alamo (pg. 50-51)
Basic Diorama Kit
- All kit contents used.

Building & Structure Kit
- Project Board
- Construction Board
- Ribbed Board
- Project Glue
- Project Sticks
- Project Wire

San Diego de Alcalá (pg. 52-54)
Desert Oasis Kit
- Palm Trees
- Desert Sand ReadyGrass Sheet
- Talus
- Yellow Flowers
- Green Grass
- Foliage Fiber
- Project Glue
- Spray Bottle
- Sticky Bond
- Foam Brush
- Stir Stick

Life Along the Nile (pg. 55-57)
Desert Oasis Diorama Kit
- All kit contents are used.

Ripplin' Water Kit
- Water Undercoat
- Realistic Water
- Foam Brush
- Stir Stick

Daily Life in Ancient Egypt (pg. 58-59)
Desert Oasis Diorama Kit
- All kit contents are used.

Building & Structure Kit
- Ribbed Board
- Project Board
- Project Cloth
- Project Sticks
- Project Glue

Pyramids of Giza (pg. 60-61)
Desert Oasis Diorama Kit
- All kit contents used.

Parthenon (pg. 62-63)

Medieval Castle (pg. 64-66)
Basic Diorama Kit
- All kit contents are used.

Building & Structure Kit
- Project Board
- Construction Board
- Project Sticks
- Project Wire
- Project Glue

Ripplin' Water Kit
- Water Undercoat
- Realistic Water
- Foam Brush
- Stir Stick

Burg Eltz (pg. 67-69)
Water Diorama Kit
- Side Panels
- Plaster Cloth
- Project Glue
- Spray Bottle
- Realistic Water
- Earth Undercoat
- Water Undercoat
- Green Grass
- Evergreen Accent
- Forest Green Accent

- Shrubs
- Talus
- Foliage Fiber
- Plastic Cup & Sifter Lid
- Stir Stick
- Foam Brush

Castle Life (pg. 70-73)
Foliage & Grasses
- All kit contents used.

Ripplin' Water Kit
- Water Undercoat
- Realistic Water
- Foam Brush
- Stir Stick

Egyptian Burial Artifacts (pg. 74-75)
Sculpting Kit
- Sculpting Clay
- Project Paints
- Project Glue
- Sculpting Tool
- Paintbrush

Medusa (pg. 76-77)
Sculpting Kit
- Sculpting Clay
- Project Paints
- Paintbrush
- Project Glue
- Sculpting Tool

Bacteria Cell (pg. 78-79)
Sculpting Kit
- Sculpting Clay
- Project Paints
- Paintbrush
- Project Glue
- Sculpting Tool
- Project Wire

Brain Cell (pg. 80-81)
Sculpting Kit
- Sculpting Clay
- Project Paints
- Paintbrush
- Project Glue
- Sculpting Tool
- Project Wire

Geysers (pg. 82-84)
Water Diorama Kit
- Side Panels
- Plaster Cloth
- Plastic Cup & Sifter Lid
- Project Glue, Spray Bo
- Realistic Water
- Earth Undercoat
- Stir Stick, Foam Brush
- Green Grass
- Evergreen Accent
- Forest Green Accent
- Shrubs
- Talus
- Foliage Fiber

Lungs and Smoking (pg. 85-87)
Ripplin' Water Kit
- Realistic Water
- Water Effects
- Stir Stick

Cross-Section Volcano (pg. 88-90)
Mountain Diorama Kit
- All kit contents are use

Energy Efficiency (pg. 91-9
Mountain Diorama Kit
- Side Panels
- Plaster Cloth
- Casting Plaster
- Rock Mold
- Mixing Tray
- Rock Colors
- Earth Undercoat
- Talus, Foliage Fiber
- Green Grass
- Evergreen Accent
- Forest Green Accent
- Shrubs
- Plastic Cup & Sifter Lid
- Spray Bottle
- Foam Brush
- Stir Stick
- Project Glue

INDEX